ANCIENT MAYA AND AZTEC CIVILIZATIONS

MARION WOOD
UPDATED BY PETER MITCHELL

THIRD EDITION

CHELSEA HOUSE
PUBLISHERS
An imprint of Infobase Publishing

Cultural Atlas for Young People
ANCIENT MAYA AND AZTEC CIVILIZATIONS
Third Edition

Copyright © 2007 The Brown Reference Group plc

Chelsea House
An imprint of Infobase Publishing
132 West 31st Street
New York, NY 10001

Library of Congress Cataloging-in-Publication Data available upon request.

ISBN: 0-8160-6820-8

ISBN 13 digit: 978-0-8160-6820-3

Set ISBN: 978-0-8160-7218-7

Chelsea House books are available at special discounts when purchased in bulk quantities for businesses, associations, institutions, or sales promotions. Please call our Special Sales Department in New York at (212) 967-8800 or (800) 322-8755.

You can find Chelsea House on the World Wide Web at:
http://www.chelseahouse.com

The Brown Reference Group
(incorporating Andromeda Oxford Limited)
8 Chapel Place, Rivington Street
London EC2A 3DQ
www.brownreference.com

For The Brown Reference Group plc:
Editorial Director: Lindsey Lowe
Project Editor: Graham Bateman
Editor: Virginia Carter
Design: Steve McCurdy
Senior Managing Editor: Tim Cooke

Printed in Singapore

10 9 8 7 6 5 4 3 2 1

Contents

Introduction

THIS BOOK IS ABOUT ANCIENT AMERICA. ALTHOUGH WE OFTEN talk of Christopher Columbus "discovering" America in 1492, prehistoric hunters in search of food had crossed into northwest America from Asia thousands of years earlier. By the time Columbus arrived, there were millions of these Native Americans. Columbus called these people Indians, because he thought that he had traveled around the world and had landed in the East Indies. In this book we use the term Native Americans rather than American Indians, but particular tribes are referred to as Indians, for example Plains and Natchez Indians.

We cannot lump together the ancient Americans as we might the ancient Greeks or ancient Romans. There were (and are) many Native American peoples, speaking separate languages and living in very different ways. In this book you will read about the most important of those that lived in the period from the end of the Ice Age to the beginning of European exploration and conquest in the late 15th century. Over these 12,000 years each group of ancient Americans developed skills and traditions best suited to their environment and its resources. Many were nomadic hunters and gatherers of wild plants. A number were farmers who lived in well-organized towns and villages. Some were skilled craftsmen, producing fine pottery or textiles or working in precious metals. Others built great cities and ruled vast empires.

How do we learn about these peoples of ancient America and their ways of life? Some of them, like the Maya and the Aztec, used picture-writing to record important events, and we can interpret this. But the majority had no form of writing at all. For the most part, therefore, we must depend on archaeological evidence, but this also varies greatly. Some ancient Americans are well represented by the remains of their stone buildings, carvings, textiles, pottery, and metalwork. Others, like the nomadic hunters who lived in skin tents or brushwood shelters, have left little trace behind. Not surprisingly, we know more about the first group than we do about the second.

Ancient Maya and Aztec Civilizations begins with a short overview of the early history of the whole of the American continent. Then the book is divided into two main sections. The first, **The History of North America**, looks in detail at the people and places of the North American subcontinent. The second section, **The History of Latin America**, deals with Mesoamerica and South America, in particular with the great civilizations such as those of the Aztecs in Mexico and the Incas in Peru.

The account of ancient American history begins in detail around 1500 B.C.E. Two terms that are used may need explanation. "Latin America" means those areas where European languages derived from Latin (such as Spanish and Portuguese) are now spoken. "Mesoamerica" refers to those parts of Mexico and Central America (from Guatemala to Panama) that had advanced cultures before the Spanish Conquest.

This book is an atlas. There are lots of maps to help you understand what was happening in different parts of America at different times. Many of the maps are accompanied by charts giving important dates or useful information. Our story is arranged in double-page spreads. Each spread is a complete story. So you can either read the book from beginning to end or just dip into it to learn about a specific topic. The Glossary on page 92 contains definitions of some of the terms used in the book. If you want to look up a particular place on a map, the Gazetteer on page 93 will tell you where to find it.

Abbreviations used in this book

B.C.E. = Before Common Era (also known as B.C.).
C.E. = Common Era (also known as A.D.). c. = *circa* (about).
in = inch; ft = foot; yd = yard; mi = mile; cu = cubic.
cm = centimeter; m = meter; km = kilometer.

▶ Pueblo Indian cliff dwellings at Mesa Verde in Colorado, North America, from about 1000 C.E.

Timelines

	1200 B.C.E.	1000 B.C.E.	800 B.C.E.	500 B.C.E.	100 B.C.E.	1 C.E.
NORTH AMERICA	Poverty Point built c.1500.	End of Archaic period c.1200–1000.	Dorset people begin to spread over eastern Arctic c.1000.	Adena people in Ohio valley c.700.	Large villages such as Ipiutak built in Alaska c.500. Woodlands farmers move westward into Plains c.250.	Hopewell people in Ohio valley c.100. Southwestern farmers (Hohokam, Mogollon, Anasazi) c.100.

Stone spearhead from Folsom, New Mexico, c.9000 B.C.E.

Clay figurine from Poverty Point, c.1500 B.C.E.

Ivory snow goggles and boss from Ipiutak, Alaska, c.500 B.C.E.–500 C.E.

MESOAMERICA	Development of Olmec civilization. San Lorenzo founded c.1500.		Olmec site of La Venta founded c.900.		Decline of Olmec civilization c.400. Development of early Maya civilization c.300.	

Carving of trophy head from Cerro Sechin, Peru, c.1300 B.C.E.

Bowl from Tlapacoya, valley of Mexico, c.1200–900 B.C.E.

Olmec head, La Venta, c.900–400 B.C.E.

SOUTH AMERICA	Oldest known metalwork c.1500.	Development of Chavín civilization c.1200.	Chavín de Huantar founded c.850.	Paracas tombs c.700–200.	Nazca people on south coast of Peru c.370 B.C.E.–450 C.E. Decline of Chavín de Huantar c.200.	Arawak Indians arrive in Antilles c.100.

Thule people appear in Alaska c.500.

Cahokia founded c.600.

Mississippi towns built c.800.

Farming villages in eastern Plains.

Chaco Canyon towns built c.900–1100.

Northern Iroquoians settle around Great Lakes c.1000.

Thule people begin to spread over eastern Arctic c.1000.

Norse settlement in Newfoundland c.1000.

Cliff dwellings at Mesa Verde and Canyon de Chelly c.1100.

Drought in Southwest 1276–99.

Cliff dwellings abandoned c.1300.

Decline of Cahokia c.1450.

Cartier explores St. Lawrence valley 1535–36.

De Soto explores Southeast 1539–42.

Coronado explores Southwest and southern Plains 1540–42.

Mica hand, Hopewell culture, 100 B.C.E.–600 C.E.

Stone paint palette from Snaketown, c.100–500 C.E.

Kneeling cat figure from Key Marco, Florida, c.800–1500 C.E.

Cliff Palace, Mesa Verde, c.1100 C.E.

Teotihuacán founded c.150.

Development of Classic Maya civilization c.300.

Reign of Pacal at Palenque 618–53.

Teotihuacán destroyed c.750.

Collapse of lowland Maya civilization c.900.

Toltec city of Tula founded c.950.

Tula destroyed 1168.

Decline of Maya civilization in Yucatán c.1200.

Aztec city of Tenochtitlán founded c.1345.

Aztecs control valley of Mexico 1428.

Aztec empire reaches greatest extent 1502.

Cortés invades Mexico 1519.

Spaniards conquer Mexico and destroy Aztec empire 1519–21.

Clay house model, Ecuador, c.500 B.C.E.–500 C.E.

Moche pot c.100–500 C.E.

Lord Chac Zutz from Palenque, 730 C.E.

Inca silver statuette, c.1400–1520 C.E.

Moche people on north coast of Peru c.1–600.

Development of Tiahuanaco and Huari c.500.

Huari abandoned c.800.

Decline of Tiahuanaco c.1000.

Carib Indians arrive in Antilles c.1200.

Inca city of Cuzco founded 1200.

Columbus lands in Bahamas 1492.

Spaniards conquer Peru and destroy Inca empire 1532.

The Land and People

THE ENTIRE LENGTH OF AMERICA MEASURES about 9,000 miles (14,500 km) from the Arctic Ocean to the tip of South America. Over this vast distance there are many changes of climate and landscape. There are icy wastes, fertile river valleys, tropical forests, grasslands, and deserts.

The Native Americans, who arrived long before European explorers, lived in different ways according to their environment.

Hunters and farmers

Some of the early Native American peoples, such as the Shoshone who lived in the deserts west of the Rocky Mountains, were nomadic hunters and gatherers, wandering in search of the animals and plants that they needed for food. They carried their few belongings on their backs and camped in simple brushwood shelters.

Others, like the Aztecs, who settled in the fertile Valley of Mexico, were farmers, living in permanent villages close to their fields. They were also fierce warriors who fought neighboring peoples and seized their lands. In time they founded a great empire that controlled a large part of Central America for 100 years.

► The Rocky Mountains and the Andes are part of the mountain chain that runs along the western side of the American continents like a giant backbone. The mountains on the eastern side are less dramatic, with the Appalachian Mountains in the north and the Brazilian Highlands in the south. In between, the land is mainly low-lying with broad valleys drained by great rivers such as the Mississippi, the Amazon, and the Orinoco.

◄ In the forests of Ecuador a mountain stream rushes to join the distant Amazon, eventually reaching the Atlantic Ocean 4,000 miles (6,400 km) away. The forest peoples were hunters and farmers. They cut down trees and burned the undergrowth to make clearings where they could plant crops and build houses. When the land was used up or exhausted, they moved on to clear another part of the forest.

◄ In this early 20th-century photo, an Inuit (Eskimo) craftsman uses old skills to make a cribbage scoreboard for sale to tourists. The Inuit, who were hunters, invented ingenious tools to help overcome their harsh environment, such as the bow drill, which was used to make holes in tough materials. Here, the string of the bow is twisted around the drill shaft which the craftsman holds in his mouth. As he moves the bow to and fro, the shaft rotates and its metal point drills into the walrus tusk.

ARCTIC OCEAN

A B C D E F

7

GREENLAND
(Denmark)

Baffin
Island

ICELAND

ALASKA

Bering Strait

Yukon Mt Mckinley
△ 20,320

ALASKA RANGE

MACKENZIE MTS

Mackenzie

Gt Bear Lake

Gt Slave Lake

L Athabasca

Hudson
Bay

6

COAST MTS

ROCKY MOUNTAINS

Great

Plains

Missouri

CANADA

L Winnipeg

L Superior

L Michigan

Ottawa

St Lawrence

Labrador

Newfoundland

Cascade Range

Sierra Nevada

Great
Basin

UNITED STATES
OF AMERICA

L Huron

L Ontario

L Erie

Ohio

APPALACHIAN MTS

Washington

5

ATLANTIC OCEAN

Sierra Madre Occidental

Rio Grande

Sierra Madre Oriental

MEXICO

Gulf of Mexico

Havana

BAHAMAS

CUBA

DOMINICAN REPUBLIC

PACIFIC OCEAN

Mississippi

Mexico City
Valley of
Mexico

Guatemala City

GUATEMALA

San Salvador
EL SALVADOR

BELIZE
Belmopan

HONDURAS

Tegucigalpa

NICARAGUA

Managua

COSTA RICA

San José

JAMAICA

HAITI

Port-au-
Prince

Santo Domingo

Puerto
Rico
(USA)

Lesser
Antilles

Caribbean Sea

TRINIDAD
AND TOBAGO

4

Panama
City

PANAMA

Caracas

VENEZUELA

Bogotá

Orinoco

GUIANA

Georgetown

GUYANA

Paramaribo

SURINAME

FRENCH
GUIANA
(France)

Feet
13,000
3,250
650
0
6,500 Sea depth

── ── International boundary

■ Capital city

△ 20,320 Mountain peak (feet)

Equatorial scale 1 : 54 000 000

COLOMBIA

Galápagos Is

Quito

ECUADOR

Japurá

Ucayali

HIGHLANDS

ANDES

Amazon

Selvas

Madeira

PERU

Lima

L Titicaca

Ancohuma
21,490

La Paz

BOLIVIA

Paraguay

Araguaia

BRAZIL

Brasília

BRAZILIAN HIGHLANDS

3

PARAGUAY

Asunción

Paraná

URUGUAY

ANDES

Aconcagua
22,834

Santiago

CHILE

ARGENTINA

Montevideo

Buenos Aires

2

Falkland Is
(UK)

1

Cape Horn

9

The First Americans

WHEN PEOPLE FIRST REACHED AMERICA, and how, is a hotly debated question among archaeologists. Finds of stone tools at Meadowcroft Rock Shelter in Pennsylvania and of an early campsite at Monte Verde in Chile suggest that it was more than 13,000 years ago, but sites of this age are still extremely rare.

Waves of migrants

It is likely that the first people to reach America came on foot from Asia during the last Ice Age when the two continents were not separated by sea as they are now, but were linked by a land bridge some 900 miles (1,440 km) wide, known to scientists as Beringia. Grazing herds of Ice Age animals such as mammoth, mastodon, caribou, and bison wandered over the grassland bridge. In pursuit came small bands of nomadic hunters, the ancestors of the Native Americans.

The migrants came in small groups, probably over a long period of time. This view is reinforced by genetic and linguistic evidence, some of which suggests that people may have been in the Americas for longer than the archaeological record shows.

Some may have traveled by boat along the Pacific coast of Alaska and Canada. But movement across the North Atlantic, though it has been suggested, is highly unlikely.

After the ice age

When the last Ice Age ended, sea levels rose as the ice sheets melted. The land bridge from Asia was submerged about 10,000 years ago and the first campsites of the migrants vanished beneath the water. Latecomers to America, such as the Inuit (see pages 20–23), had to cross from Asia by boat.

By then other hunting groups had spread far south. Traces of their temporary campsites include chipped stone points, such as those named for the New Mexico sites of Clovis and Folsom, and Topper in South Carolina. By around 10,000 B.C.E., people had reached the southernmost tip of South America.

As the climate changed and forests replaced grasslands in many areas, large grazing animals such as the mammoth died out.

▼ Stone spearheads like this were used by the first Americans to hunt large animals. Some have been found among the bones of animals killed by people more than 10,000 years ago, about the time the last Ice Age ended.

◀ The first people to inhabit the cold plains of Ice Age America were small bands of nomadic hunters. The animals they hunted with their stone-tipped spears provided food for their families, as well as skins for tents and for warm clothing.

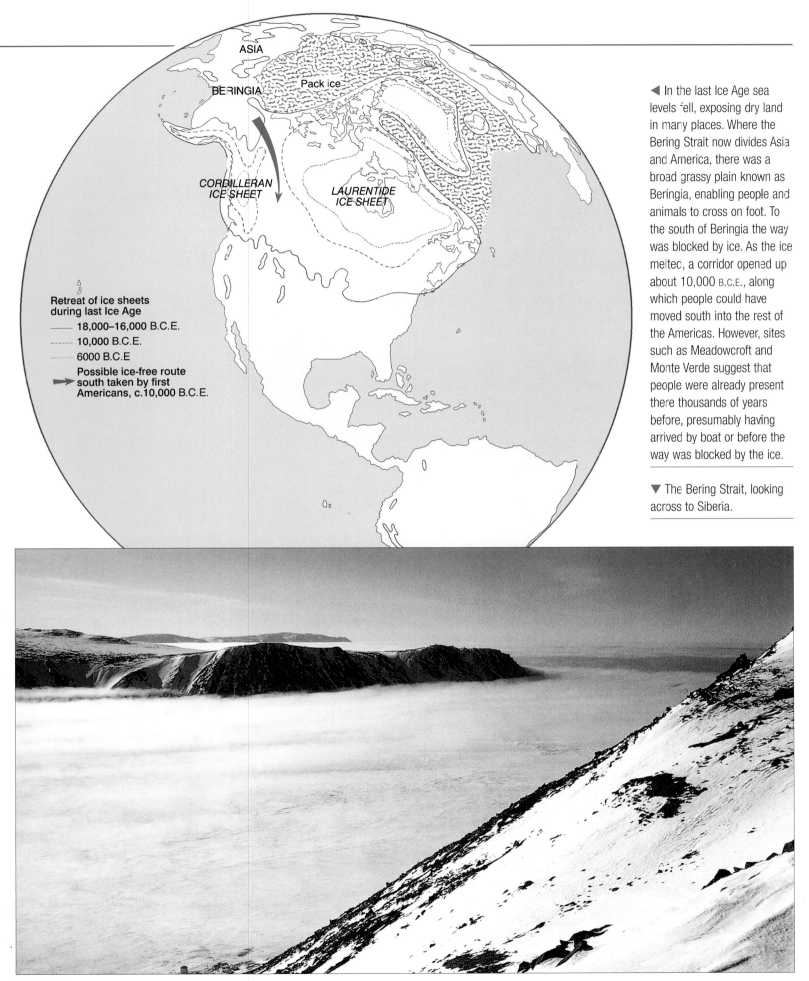

ASIA

BERINGIA

Pack ice

CORDILLERAN
ICE SHEET

LAURENTIDE
ICE SHEET

Retreat of ice sheets
during last Ice Age

—— 18,000–16,000 B.C.E.

----- 10,000 B.C.E.

········· 6000 B.C.E

➤ Possible ice-free route
south taken by first
Americans, c.10,000 B.C.E.

◀ In the last Ice Age sea levels fell, exposing dry land in many places. Where the Bering Strait now divides Asia and America, there was a broad grassy plain known as Beringia, enabling people and animals to cross on foot. To the south of Beringia the way was blocked by ice. As the ice melted, a corridor opened up about 10,000 B.C.E., along which people could have moved south into the rest of the Americas. However, sites such as Meadowcroft and Monte Verde suggest that people were already present there thousands of years before, presumably having arrived by boat or before the way was blocked by the ice.

▼ The Bering Strait, looking across to Siberia.

Exploration and Conquest

VIKINGS FROM NORSE SETTLEMENTS in Greenland explored the Labrador and Newfoundland coasts about 1000 C.E. They settled at L'Anse aux Meadows, but later they returned to Greenland.

Columbus and the *conquistadores*

In 1492 Christopher Columbus landed in the Bahamas. He claimed these islands for the king and queen of Spain. Mistakenly believing that he had found a new route to India, he called the Native Americans "Indians." Columbus's voyages opened the way for European exploration and conquest.

All the Caribbean islands were soon under Spanish rule. From their base in Hispaniola, the *conquistadores* launched a series of invasions of the mainland. In 1519–21 Hernán Cortés conquered Mexico and destroyed the Aztec empire. In 1533 the Inca empire in Peru fell to Spanish forces led by Francisco Pizarro.

Several Spanish expeditions explored the southern parts of North America, hoping to find rich cities like those in Mexico and Peru.

Hernando de Soto, who had served under Pizarro in Peru, landed in Florida in 1539. He spent many months exploring the southeast, attacking and looting Native American villages. In 1541 he reached the Mississippi, but he died the following year.

In 1540–42 Francisco de Coronado and his men explored the southwest and the southern plains as far as Kansas. They captured several Native American villages but did not find the treasure they had hoped for. They returned to Mexico disappointed and empty-handed.

◄ An Eastern Woodlands hunter painted by a 16th-century English explorer. He hunted chiefly buffalo and deer and wears a buffalo-skin breechcloth. His face and body are painted. A wristguard protects his arm from the bowstring. His quiver is slung over his shoulder.

▼ Columbus landing in the Bahamas in what Europeans called the New World. The Bahamas islanders were the Arawak. Sadly, their fate was to be typical— slavery, exile, and death from disease and ill-treatment by their conquerors.

► Many early explorers, such as Ferdinand Magellan from Portugal and Francis Drake from England, sailed along the coasts and did not venture far inland. When explorers began to invade, fighting often broke out, and hundreds of Native Americans were killed. Many others died of European diseases against which they had no resistance. As a result, the Native American population fell dramatically during the 16th century. In Latin America many people are of mixed Native American and European descent. They are known as *mestizos*.

Jacques Cartier claimed land along the St. Lawrence River for France in the 1530s, but settlement of North America by Europeans did not get underway until the following century.

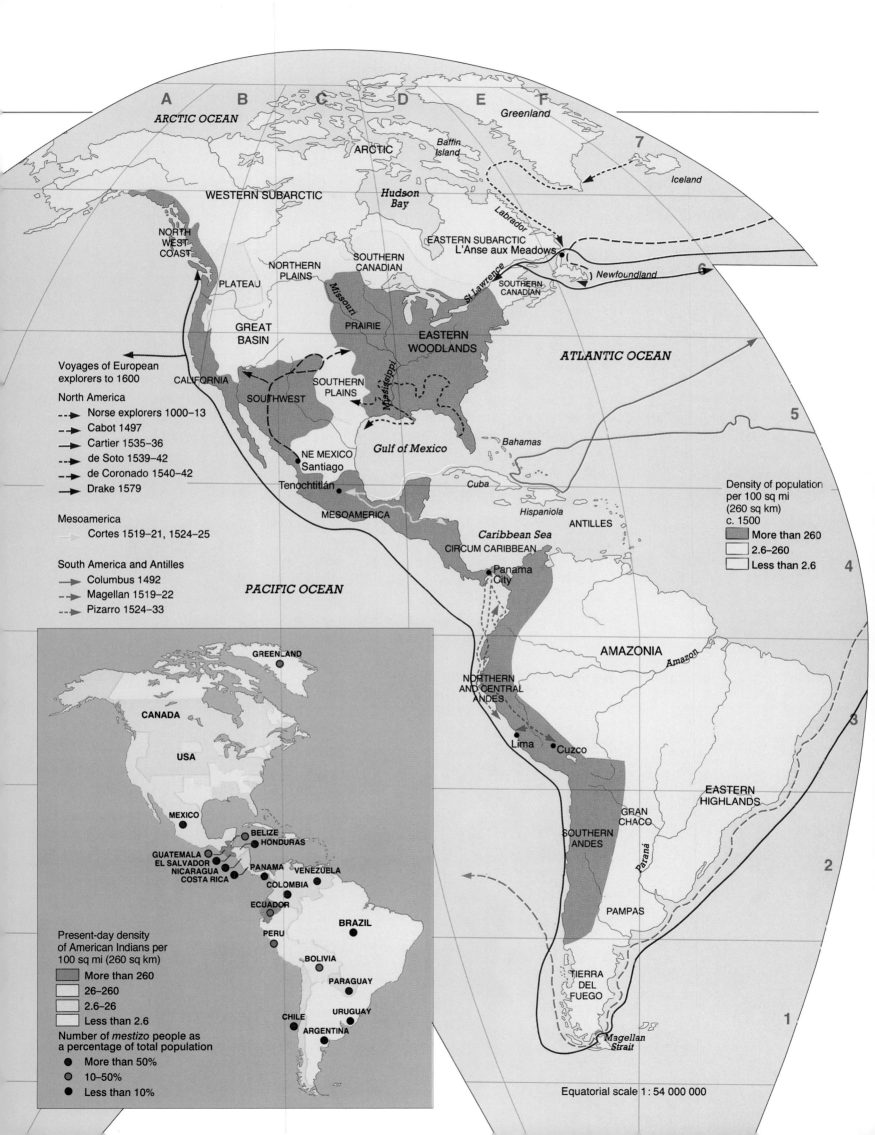

ARCTIC OCEAN

A B C D E F

Greenland

ARCTIC

Baffin Island

Iceland

WESTERN SUBARCTIC

Hudson Bay

7

NORTH WEST COAST

NORTHERN PLAINS

SOUTHERN CANADIAN

EASTERN SUBARCTIC
L'Anse aux Meadows

Labrador

PLATEAU

GREAT BASIN

PRAIRIE

Missouri

SOUTHERN CANADIAN

Newfoundland

6

EASTERN WOODLANDS

St Lawrence

ATLANTIC OCEAN

CALIFORNIA

SOUTHWEST

SOUTHERN PLAINS

Mississippi

Voyages of European explorers to 1600

North America
- - -→ Norse explorers 1000–13
——→ Cabot 1497
——→ Cartier 1535–36
- - -→ de Soto 1539–42
- - -→ de Coronado 1540–42
——→ Drake 1579

NE MEXICO
Santiago

Tenochtitlán

Gulf of Mexico

Bahamas

5

Cuba

MESOAMERICA

Hispaniola

ANTILLES

Mesoamerica
——→ Cortes 1519–21, 1524–25

Caribbean Sea

CIRCUM CARIBBEAN

Density of population per 100 sq mi (260 sq km) c. 1500

More than 260
2.6–260
Less than 2.6

South America and Antilles
——→ Columbus 1492
- - -→ Magellan 1519–22
- - -→ Pizarro 1524–33

Panama City

4

PACIFIC OCEAN

AMAZONIA

Amazon

NORTHERN AND CENTRAL ANDES

Lima

Cuzco

3

EASTERN HIGHLANDS

GRAN CHACO

SOUTHERN ANDES

Paraná

2

PAMPAS

TIERRA DEL FUEGO

1

Magellan Strait

Equatorial scale 1 : 54 000 000

GREENLAND

CANADA

USA

MEXICO

BELIZE
HONDURAS

GUATEMALA
EL SALVADOR
NICARAGUA
COSTA RICA

PANAMA

VENEZUELA

COLOMBIA

ECUADOR

PERU

BRAZIL

BOLIVIA

PARAGUAY

URUGUAY

CHILE

ARGENTINA

Present-day density of American Indians per 100 sq mi (260 sq km)

More than 260
26–260
2.6–26
Less than 2.6

Number of *mestizo* people as a percentage of total population

● More than 50%
◐ 10–50%
● Less than 10%

Part One

The History of North America

▲ Feathered man, from a Southern Cult engraved shell dating from about 1100 C.E. The design reflects the Hopewell people's customs and beliefs but also has Mexican influences.

▶ Mount McKinley, now known as often by its Native American name Denali ("the great one") rises 20,320 ft (6,200 m) above central Alaska. This part of the Arctic was the homeland of the Athapascan people for thousands of years.

North America: Land and Climate

ALTHOUGH THE FAR NORTH OF THE continent is cold throughout the year, most of North America has a temperate climate. There are cold winters, warm or hot summers, and pleasant spring and fall seasons. The rainfall varies. Most rain falls over the mountain ranges and along the coasts. Over the great central plain the climate is drier and in some areas, such as the southwest, the land is semidesert or desert.

Coasts and forests

The Arctic landscape changes from ice and snow in the far north to the cold treeless plain known as the tundra, inhabited by the Inuit. Farther south, and stretching along the north Pacific coast, lie dense forests of pine, spruce, and cedar. On the other side of the country, from the Great Lakes south to the Gulf of Mexico, the land is also wooded, with some evergreens including spruce and fir. But broad-leaved deciduous trees such as birch and oak are more common. The groups of people who made up the Eastern Woodlands culture dwelt here and formed prosperous farming communities (see pages 18–19 and 24–25).

Grasslands and buffalo

Between the Rocky Mountains and the Mississippi River lies the area known as the Great Plains. The western or High Plains were dry and windswept with short coarse grass. But on the eastern prairies, the grass was thick and tall, growing nearly 7 feet (2.1 m) high. Great buffalo herds, up to several million strong, once grazed here. By the end of the 19th century, due to overhunting by white hunters, buffalo were almost extinct. Today much of the land is cultivated, and wheat and corn are grown over vast areas.

Southwestern deserts

Southwest of the Plains the land rises to form a high sandstone plateau cut by deep canyons. Rainfall is low here, but Native American farmers were able to grow corn and other crops by digging irrigation channels to water their fields.

West of the Rocky Mountains lies the Great Basin, the most barren area of North America. Today modern irrigation has made farming here possible, but in prehistoric times it was too dry for Native American methods of agriculture.

◀ The coast of southeastern Alaska near the town of Juneau. During the last Ice Age the area was covered with sheets of ice, remnants of which still exist as glaciers in some mountain valleys.

▼ Canyon de Chelly, east of the Grand Canyon in Arizona. This landscape was sculpted by rivers when the climate was much wetter. Windblown sand has eroded the softer rock into strange shapes.

▶ The different types of natural environment found in North America have evolved over the past 10,000 years (after the last Ice Age ended). Changes in climate at various times have affected both plant and animal life.

As deserts appeared or as forests replaced grassland, some kinds of animals moved to other areas in search of new sources of food. Others died out altogether.

In turn, such changes affected the way people lived. Some people turned to hunting other animals and moved to new areas in pursuit of them. Others began to gather more wild plants and vegetables and in time became farmers.

Sometimes prehistoric peoples tried to alter the landscape themselves in order to improve their way of life. Hunters set fire to areas of forest to provide better grazing for the deer they hunted. Woodland farmers used fire to clear land for cultivation. In dry areas some dug irrigation channels to grow crops.

▶ The Yellowstone River near its source in the foothills of the Rocky Mountains. From here it flows through the northern Plains to join the Missouri River. Huge herds of buffalo once grazed in this area.

ARCTIC OCEAN

Greenland

Iceland

Bering Strait

Yukon

Mackenzie

Great Bear Lake

Great Slave Lake

Hudson Bay

ROCKY MOUNTAINS

Fraser

PACIFIC OCEAN

Great Plains

L Winnipeg

L Superior

L Huron

St Lawrence

L Ontario

L Michigan

L Erie

Missouri

Great Basin

Eastern Woodlands

APPALACHIAN MTS

Arkansas

Ohio

Colorado

Mississippi

ATLANTIC OCEAN

Rio Grande

Sierra Madre Occidental

Sierra Madre Oriental

Gulf of Mexico

Tundra and Ice
Coniferous forest
Mixed forest
Tropical rainforest
Grass and
Semidesert and scrub
Desert

Scale 1 : 40 000 000
0   800 km
0   600 miles

17

North America After the Ice

BY 8000 B.C.E. MOST OF THE BIG GAME animals such as the horse, mammoth, and mastodon had died out. People turned to hunting a wider range of smaller animals. Since they no longer needed to follow the big game herds, their way of life became less nomadic.

They began to restrict their wanderings to particular areas and to make the most of the various sources of food found there at different times of the year. They began to collect more wild plants for food, although they did not yet grow their own crops. This period is known as the Archaic.

Hunting and fishing

The most important animals for Archaic hunters were deer and caribou. They provided large amounts of meat, and their skins could be turned into clothing and other useful items. But smaller game was also

hunted, for example, rabbits, otters, beavers, raccoons, and several kinds of birds. In addition, the sea, lakes, and rivers supplied a whole variety of fish and shellfish.

As people varied their activities, they began to use more specialized weapons and tools. Stone-tipped spears were still the hunter's favorite weapon. Sometimes he used a spear thrower, which helped him hurl his spear with more force than if he simply

▼ After the Ice Age, the climate and landscape became similar to those of today. People began to follow new ways of life. Some remained nomadic, constantly on the move in search of food. But in areas where there were plenty of animals and plants to eat, many people chose to remain in one place at least for part of the year. This map shows some of the places where they settled.

Life in the Archaic period 8000–1000 B.C.E.
Subarctic Hunting, fishing, and gathering people, small campsites.
Eastern Woodlands Hunting and gathering people, living in winter villages and traveling to summer campsites.
Plains Nomadic buffalo hunters, small campsites.
Northwest coast Hunting and fishing people, winter villages, and summer campsites.
Southwestern deserts Hunting and gathering, fishing along coast, cave shelters, and campsites.

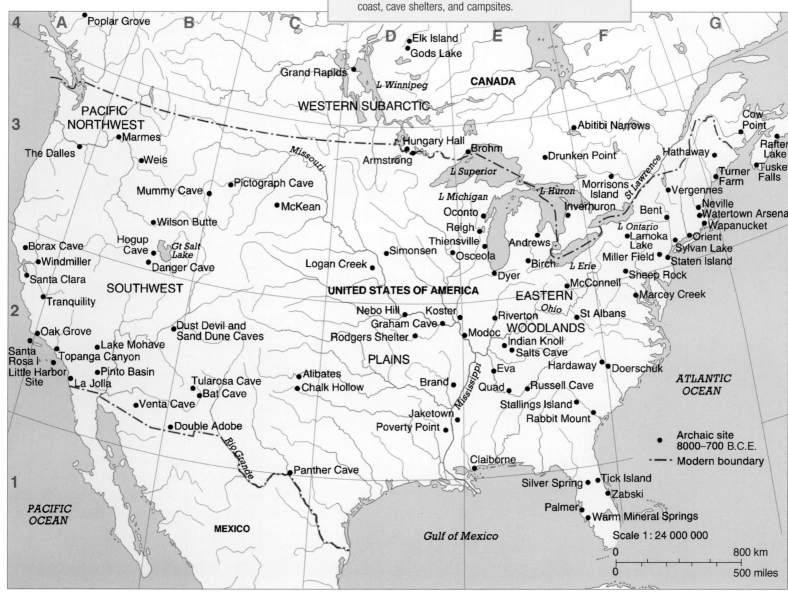

◀ ▶ Danger Cave lies on the edge of the Great Salt Lake Desert in Utah. Bands of hunter-gatherers camped here from about 9000 B.C.E. and left many belongings behind. Even items that normally perish, such as food, clothing, and baskets, have survived in the dry desert climate—so much so that by 2,000 years ago the cave was blocked by a pile of debris 14 ft (4 m) high.

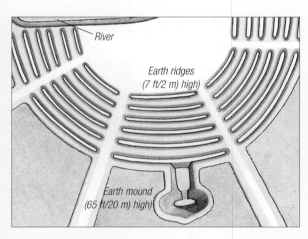

River

Earth ridges (7 ft/2 m) high)

Earth mound (65 ft/20 m) high)

Poverty Point

Poverty Point

At Poverty Point, Louisiana, a large village grew up about 1500 B.C.E. Huts were built along the top of six huge human-made ridges of earth, set one within the other (above left). The outermost ridge is 4,300 ft (1,300 m) across. The village people were hunters and fishermen.

Thousands of roughly shaped balls of clay have been found at Poverty Point. The villagers used them to cook their food. They first heated them in a fire and then dropped them into their cooking water to bring it to the required temperature. Some of the clay balls still bear fingermarks of their makers. Small clay figures (left) have also been found.

threw it by hand (see page 21). He also made nets, traps, and snares with which to catch small mammals, birds, and fish.

Using plants

People collected many kinds of fruit, seeds, and nuts according to the season. Grinding stones were used to crush or grind seeds and nuts into coarse flour, perhaps for making bread or porridge. From about 2500 B.C.E. people in the Midwest also began growing some plants, such as squashes, sunflowers, and goosefoot, although hunting, fishing, and gathering wild foods continued to provide most of their diet.

People wove baskets, mats, and bags from grass and reeds. Baskets were also coated with clay and may have been used to boil food—the water was heated by dropping hot stones or balls of clay inside. This method of cooking, known as "stone boiling," continued in parts of North America up until 100 years ago, but in the eastern United States pottery came into use from about 2500 B.C.E.

Following the seasons

People moved according to the season, often following a set pattern. They had special places where they returned year after year. In the Eastern Woodlands people lived in permanent base camps or villages during the winter and returned there after long hunting trips in summer.

People who lived in the southwestern deserts moved from one cave shelter to another during the year. Often they left heavy tools and food supplies at each spot so that they did not have to carry too much with them as they traveled.

The Arctic

THE ANCESTORS OF TODAY'S INUIT (see page 22) were the last native people to move into North America from Asia in about 4000 B.C.E. From Alaska they spread eastward along the central Arctic coast, reaching Greenland by about 2500 B.C.E. Most modern Inuit are probably distant descendants of these people.

The early Inuit were all nomadic hunters and fishermen. Some of their campsites have revealed small, finely worked tools and weapons, and bones of the animals they hunted.

The eastern Arctic

The Dorset people, who take their name from Cape Dorset on Baffin Island, spread over much of Canada and Greenland from about 1000 B.C.E. They were hunters of seal, walrus, and caribou. In summer they went on long hunting trips, living in skin tents. Although they had invented sleds, they had no dogs. They had to haul their equipment themselves. During the winter months they lived in villages. Their houses, partly underground for warmth, had walls of turf covered with skins. Inside each house there was an open hearth or fireplace in the middle of the floor, and around the walls were benches for people to sit or sleep on.

The western Arctic

From about 500 B.C.E. large villages were built along the Alaskan coast. Ipiutak on Point Hope perhaps had 700 houses. Many beautiful walrus bone and ivory carvings have been found in the burial ground at Ipiutak. For hunting seal and walrus, the Alaskan (Okvik) people used kayaks, light canoes made by stretching skins over a wooden framework. They also hunted whales, using larger open boats called *umiaks*, and used dogs to pull their sleds. These people were skilled carvers in ivory.

Thule, the name the Romans gave to the far north, is also the name given to late prehistoric Arctic peoples. The Thule people of Alaska were ingenious hunters who invented new types of harpoons and boats for hunting sea mammals, especially whales.

Around 1000 C.E. the Thule people began to move eastward, perhaps seizing territory by force and conquering the inhabitants. Inuit legends tell of an earlier race of giants, the Tunit, who were driven away after fierce battles with Inuit ancestors. These tales may refer to encounters of the Dorset and Thule peoples.

▼ Most Inuit have always lived along the coasts of the tundra region, the treeless land beyond the northern limits of forest. The animals they hunted supplied them with all their needs. Over thousands of years they perfected a way of life that is ideally suited to the harsh Arctic environment.

Settlement in the Arctic 4000 B.C.E.–1500 C.E.

c.4000–3000 B.C.E. The first Inuit begin to move into America from Asia.

c.2000 B.C.E. Inuit people reach northernmost Greenland.

c.1000 B.C.E.–1000 C.E. The Dorset people spread over the eastern Arctic.

c.500 B.C.E.–500 C.E. Large villages like Ipiutak are built along the coast of western Alaska.

c.100 B.C.E.–100 C.E. Okvik people settle in northern Alaska.

c.500–1000 C.E. The Thule people appear in Alaska and spread all across the northern Arctic to Greenland.

c.985 Norse settlers arrive in Greenland.

c.1000–1500 The Thule people spread across the Arctic from Alaska to Greenland.

c.1400 Norse settlements in Greenland are abandoned.

Inuit (Eskimo) sites
- ◉ 4000–2000 B.C.E.
- ⊙ 2000–1000 B.C.E.
- ◉ 1000 B.C.E.–500 C.E.
- ● 500–1800 C.E.

—— Limit of permanent ice cover
– – Limit of pack ice in sea
- - - Northern limit of trees

Scale 1 : 24 000 000
0 ———————— 800 km
0 ———————— 500 miles

Inuit hunting tools

The Inuit used several kinds of harpoons and spears. A walrus harpoon had to be very strong to pierce the animal's thick hide. Spears for hunting seals and birds were smaller and lighter. Hunters used wooden spear throwers (right) to increase the spear's power. Each one was specially made for the hunter using it—its length equaled the distance between his forefinger and his elbow and in effect gave him an extra arm joint.

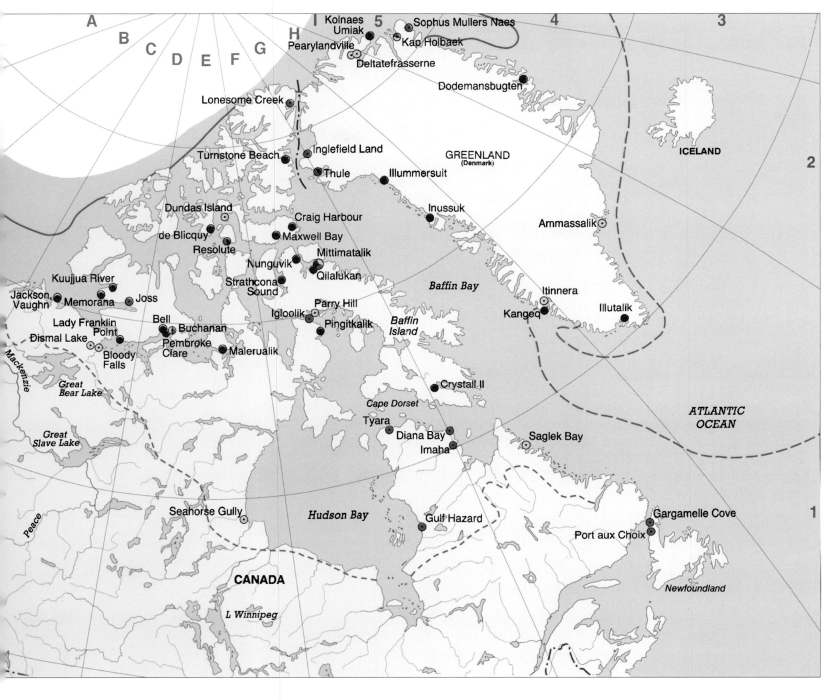

A B C D E F G H I 5 4 3

Kolnaes
Umiak
Pearylandville
Sophus Mullers Naes
Kap Holbaek
Deltatefrasserne
Dodemansbugten

Lonesome Creek

GREENLAND
(Denmark)

ICELAND

2

Turnstone Beach
Inglefield Land
Thule
Illummersuit

Dundas Island
Inussuk

Craig Harbour
de Blicquy
Maxwell Bay
Resolute
Mittimatalik
Nunguvik
Qilalukan
Strathcona Sound
Ammassalik

Kuujjua River
Parry Hill
Igloolik
Pingitkalik
Baffin Bay
Itinnera
Illutalik

Jackson, Vaughn
Memorana
Joss
Baffin Island
Kangeq

Lady Franklin Point
Bell
Buchanan
Dismal Lake
Pembroke
Clare
Malerualik
Bloody Falls

Great Bear Lake

Crystall II

Cape Dorset

Great Slave Lake

Tyara
Diana Bay
Imaha
Saglek Bay

ATLANTIC OCEAN

Mackenzie

Peace

Seahorse Gully
Hudson Bay
Gulf Hazard
Gargamelle Cove
Port aux Choix

1

CANADA

Newfoundland

L Winnipeg

Inuit Life

UNTIL THE BEGINNING OF THE 20TH century, the Inuit lived much as they had done for 1,000 years. They depended for all their needs on success in hunting. Their whole way of life was geared to the seasonal movements of animals such as seal and caribou.

In winter, seals were harpooned at their breathing holes in the ice. Great patience was needed. A hunter might have to stand motionless for hours, his harpoon at the ready, waiting for a seal to come up for air. In spring and summer the seals came out of the water to sun themselves on the ice. Hunters, making seal-like movements and noises, could crawl close to them before throwing their harpoons.

Late summer was the main caribou hunting season. By then the animals were well fed, providing a supply of meat to store for the long winter months. Groups of hunters came together at camps near the caribou grazing grounds. They would all ambush the herds with bows and arrows. Meat was often eaten raw, because fuel for cooking fires was scarce.

Protection from extreme cold

Warm clothing was just as important as food for survival. Sealskin was generally used for summer clothing, but in winter caribou skin was preferred. It was very warm, yet light to wear. Other skins used included those of musk oxen, polar bears, and birds. Women skinned the animals and cleaned the hides. They made all their family's clothing, stitching the skins with bone needles and gut thread. Both men and women wore hooded tunics, or "parkas," and trousers over long boots. Women's tunics often had a very large hood for carrying a baby inside.

Inuit life today

With the growth of oil and mining industries, many changes have come to the Arctic. Today, many Inuit work in these industries, live in modern houses, and eat store-bought foods. Hunters now use guns and snowmobiles. But these changes have also had undesirable outcomes, including serious problems with alcohol and diseases such as diabetes.

The Inuit remain proud of their traditions and have struggled to assert their rights to the land, particularly in Canada, where the new territory of Nunavut ("Our Land") has an Inuit majority. Its leaders and those of other Inuit are campaigning strongly to control global warming, which is already having massive and damaging effects on the climate and animals on which they depend.

▶ An Inuit fisherman bobs a lure at the edge of the ice to attract fish. He will catch them using his leister, a type of fishing spear like the one in the foreground. The fish is impaled on the central spike, and the side pieces keep it from wriggling free.

▼ Inuit in the Baffin Bay area still use dog teams for pulling sleds and other heavy loads. Here hunters are using their dogs to haul the carcasses of walruses they have just killed. A dog team may consist of as many as 14 animals harnessed in a "fan" formation. In most other areas motor sleds have replaced dog teams.

▶ ▼ Many Inuit used to live in tents of seal or caribou skin draped over frameworks of wood or bone and weighted down with stones. When winter came, they built houses of stones covered with turf. Although "igloo" is an Inuit word for any kind of house, it has come to mean one made of snow.

The Inuit built these snow houses as temporary shelters when traveling in winter. They cut blocks of hard-packed snow and arranged them in a circle. More blocks were laid on top, rising in a spiral to form a dome. The last block at the top was fitted by a man working from inside. He then cut his way out and formed the entrance tunnel.

The Burial Mound Builders

B Y ABOUT 1000 B.C.E., WELL-ORGANIZED farming communities were established in the Eastern Woodlands. As well as gathering wild plants for food, the people grew crops in fields near their villages. The Adena lived in the Ohio valley from about 700 B.C.E. They hunted, fished, and grew a number of food crops, such as squash, gourds, and sunflowers (for both seeds and roots). The Hopewell people who came after them around 100 B.C.E. grew corn as well. Their culture reached along the Mississippi River and its tributaries.

Earthworks and burial mounds

The Adena and Hopewell farmers enjoyed a settled and prosperous way of life. The huge earthworks that they built can still be seen today. Those built by the Hopewell people are especially large and elaborate. Some are enclosures, perhaps built for holding important ceremonies. Others are burial mounds, each containing log tombs where the dead were

▶ The Adena and Hopewell peoples set up trading links with distant people and places in order to obtain the raw materials that they needed, such as mica, copper, and shells. Traders traveled to these outlying places to exchange finished goods for raw materials. The people who had acquired these goods began to make copies of them and to follow the customs of their makers. This was how the way of life of the Adena and Hopewell peoples spread far beyond the Ohio valley.

◀ This hand is cut from mica, a mineral found in rocks which is then split into transparent sheets. It may have been a badge of office or used to decorate clothing.

▼ Serpent Mound earthwork in Ohio, dated to around 1070 C.E., is attributed to the Fort Ancient culture.

Trading links across North America

Raw materials used by the Adena and Hopewell peoples came from far-flung communities:

Stone from various areas for making tools, weapons, and tobacco pipes.

Copper and silver from the Great Lakes for making jewelry and musical instruments.

Mica from the Appalachian Mountains for making cutouts, shaped like hands, claws, and snakes.

Obsidian from the Rocky Mountains, a glasslike rock for making knives and spearheads.

Shells and alligator teeth from the Gulf of Mexico for making necklaces.

Pottery from south of the Appalachians.

buried with a rich array of beautiful objects. These grave offerings include necklaces, bracelets, and ear ornaments made of gold, silver, copper, pearls, and shell. There are polished stone tobacco pipes in the form of people or birds, stone and copper tools, and strange shapes cut from sheets of copper and mica.

Trading networks

The objects found in the burial mounds were made from rare and precious materials by skilled craftsmen. Many of the materials came from far away. They were imported via a network of trade routes stretching hundreds of miles along rivers and tracks from the Great Lakes in the north to the Gulf of Mexico in the south, and west to the Rocky Mountains.

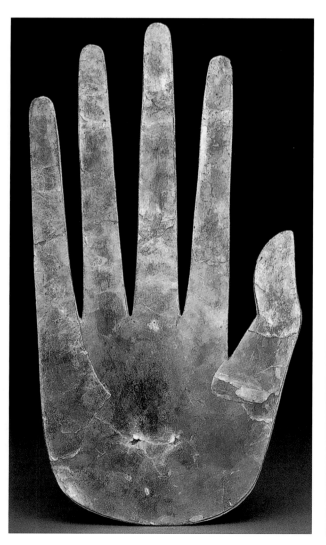

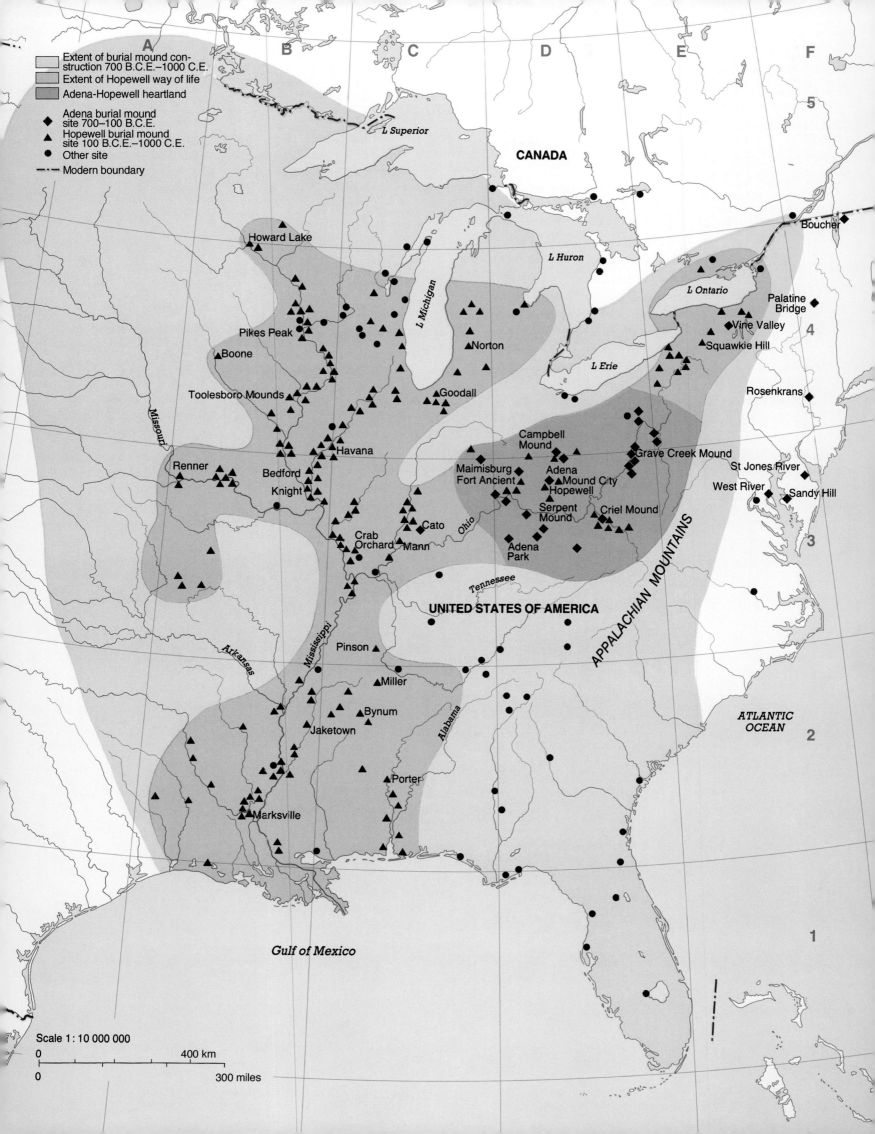

A B C D E F

5

Legend
- Extent of burial mound construction 700 B.C.E.–1000 C.E.
- Extent of Hopewell way of life
- Adena-Hopewell heartland

- ◆ Adena burial mound site 700–100 B.C.E.
- ▲ Hopewell burial mound site 100 B.C.E.–1000 C.E.
- ● Other site
- Modern boundary

L Superior

CANADA

L Huron

Boucher ◆

L Ontario

Palatine ◆
Bridge

Howard Lake ▲

L Michigan

Vine Valley ◆
Squawkie Hill ▲

4

Pikes Peak ●

▲ Norton

Rosenkrans ◆

Boone ▲

L Erie

Toolesboro Mounds

Goodall ●

Campbell
Mound ●

Grave Creek Mound ◆

St Jones River ◆

Havana ▲

Maimisburg ◆
Fort Ancient

Adena ◆
▲ Mound City

West River ●

Sandy Hill ◆

Renner ●

Bedford ▲

Hopewell ◆

Knight ▲

Serpent
Mound

Criel Mound ◆

Missouri

Cato ◆

Ohio

3

Crab
Orchard ▲
Mann

Adena ◆
Park

Tennessee

APPALACHIAN MOUNTAINS

Arkansas

Mississippi

UNITED STATES OF AMERICA

Pinson ▲

Miller ▲

Alabama

Bynum ▲

*ATLANTIC
OCEAN*

2

Jaketown

Porter ▲

Marksville ▲

1

Gulf of Mexico

Scale 1 : 10 000 000

0 ————————— 400 km

0 ————————— 300 miles

The Temple Mound Builders

AROUND 800 C.E., EASTERN WOODLAND farmers began to grow a stronger, more productive type of corn imported from Mexico. In some sheltered areas it could be planted and harvested twice in the same season. Better farming methods led to a new and wealthy way of life which is known as the Mississippian.

Mississippian settlements were larger than any built before by northern Native Americans. With thousands of inhabitants, they are considered the first real towns in North America. A typical town consisted of a number of rectangular flat-topped mounds grouped around a plaza or square. The mounds were built of earth with a ramp or stairway of logs leading to the summit. Temples and houses were built on top.

The Southern Cult

Many objects, such as shell disks and copper sheets engraved with strange designs, have been found in temple mounds in the southern Mississippian area. Designs include crosses, suns, weeping eyes, and hands with an eye in the center of the palm. They seem to be symbols of the Southern Cult, a mysterious religion about which very little is known.

▲ A chest ornament, or gorget, made of shell, engraved with a man's head. It may have been a Southern Cult object.

▼ Important people were often buried under floors of temples built on flat-topped mounds. Others were buried in cemeteries near the towns. Grave goods—pottery and shell or copper gorgets—were placed around the bodies.

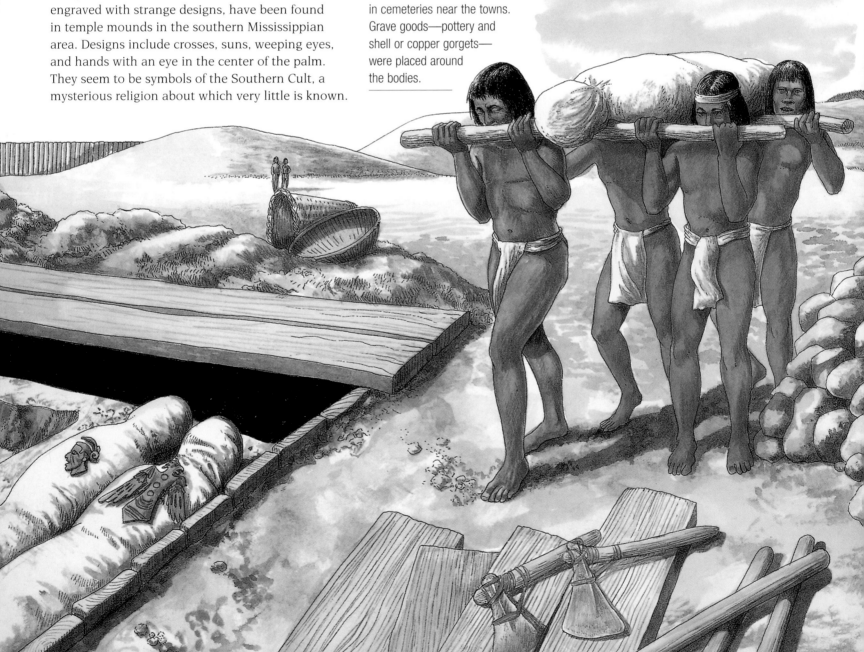

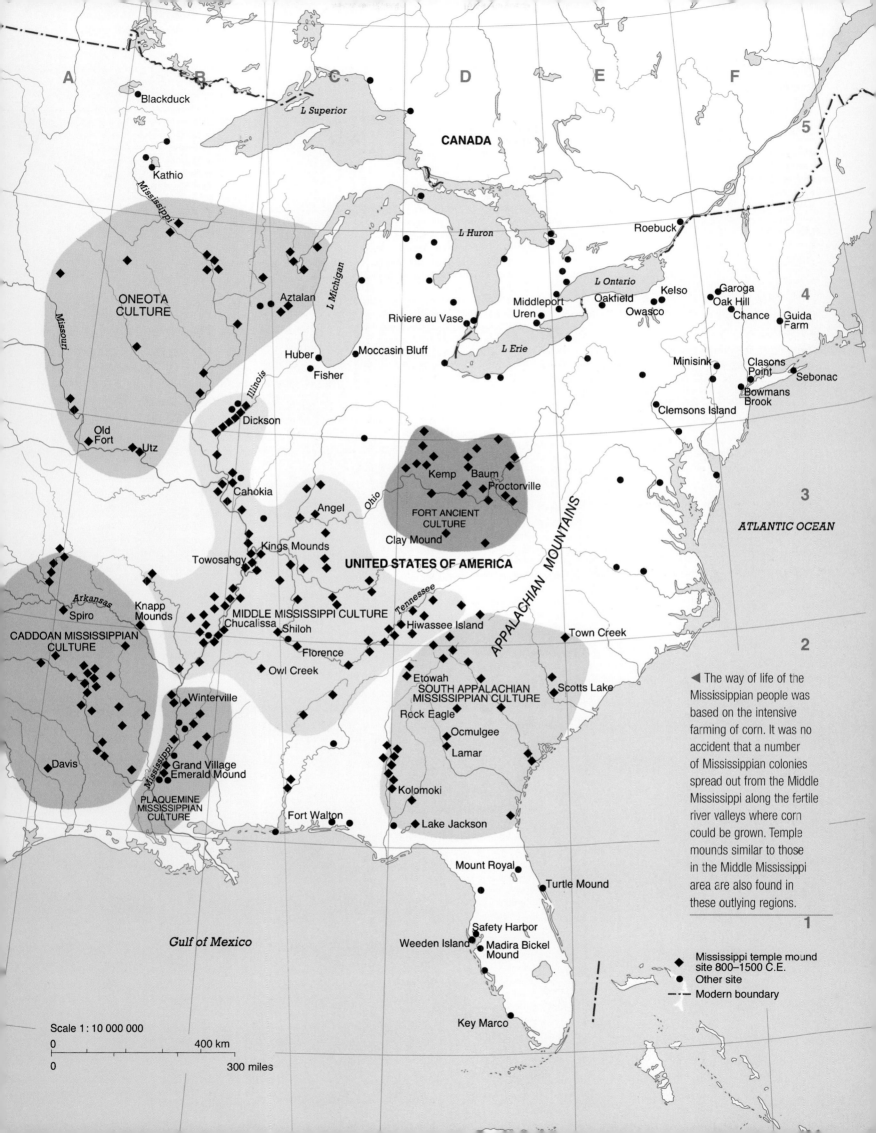

A B C D E F

5

Blackduck

L Superior

CANADA

Kathio

Mississippi

Missouri

L Huron

Roebuck

4

L Michigan

ONEOTA
CULTURE

Aztalan

L Ontario

Kelso

Garoga

Oak Hill

Middleport
Uren

Oakfield

Chance

Guida
Farm

Riviere au Vase

Owasco

Huber

Moccasin Bluff

L Erie

Minisink

Clasons
Point

Sebonac

Fisher

Bowmans
Brook

Illinois

Dickson

Clemsons Island

Old
Fort

Utz

Kemp

Baum

Proctorville

3

Cahokia

Angel

Ohio

FORT ANCIENT
CULTURE

ATLANTIC OCEAN

Clay Mound

Kings Mounds

UNITED STATES OF AMERICA

Towosahgy

Tennessee

APPALACHIAN MOUNTAINS

Arkansas

Knapp
Mounds

MIDDLE MISSISSIPPI CULTURE

Spiro

Chucalissa
Shiloh

Hiwassee Island

Town Creek

2

CADDOAN MISSISSIPPIAN
CULTURE

Florence

Owl Creek

Etowah

Scotts Lake

SOUTH APPALACHIAN
MISSISSIPPIAN CULTURE

Winterville

Rock Eagle

Davis

Mississippi

Grand Village
Emerald Mound

Ocmulgee

Lamar

◄ The way of life of the
Mississippian people was
based on the intensive
farming of corn. It was no
accident that a number
of Mississippian colonies
spread out from the Middle
Mississippi along the fertile
river valleys where corn
could be grown. Temple
mounds similar to those
in the Middle Mississippi
area are also found in
these outlying regions.

PLAQUEMINE
MISSISSIPPIAN
CULTURE

Kolomoki

Fort Walton

Lake Jackson

Mount Royal

1

Gulf of Mexico

Turtle Mound

Safety Harbor

Weeden Island

Madira Bickel
Mound

◆ Mississippi temple mound
site 800–1500 C.E.

● Other site

–·– Modern boundary

Scale 1 : 10 000 000

0   400 km

0   300 miles

Key Marco

Mound Sites

Cahokia—Mississippian mound city

CAHOKIA LIES NEAR THE MODERN CITY OF St. Louis. Founded about 600 C.E., Cahokia was the largest prehistoric city north of Mexico. In its heyday, about 1100 C.E., as many as 10,000 people may have lived there.

Cahokia contains more than 100 human-made mounds of various shapes and sizes. The largest, Monk's Mound, is a flat-topped pyramid rising in four terraces to a height of 100 feet (30 m) above the surrounding valley. Its builders had no carts or pack animals, but carried the earth there themselves in baskets.

About 1200 a wooden fence was put up around the central plaza, enclosing Monk's Mound and 16 smaller mounds. Wooden buildings on mounds were probably temples and houses of important people. Some of the mounds contained burials. Smaller mounds outside the fence may have been

▼ Cahokia consists of more than 100 mounds grouped around plazas or squares. Monk's Mound is one of the largest human-made earthworks in North America. It contains about 780,000 cubic yards (600,000 cu. m) of earth, and at its base measures 990 x 660 ft (300 x 200 m)—more than 12 times the area of a modern soccer field.

for houses and burials of less important people. Pits excavated during the construction of the mounds were used for water storage.

Government and trade

Until its decline in about 1450, Cahokia was probably the seat of government for the surrounding area. Several smaller towns were strung along the banks of the Mississippi and the other rivers that flowed into it near Cahokia. The city was also an important trading center. Grave goods that have been found in burial mounds there include copper items from the Great Lakes, mica from the Appalachians, and shells from the eastern seaboard.

▲ ▶ Small hamlets of wattle and daub houses (right) were scattered over the fertile river plain around Cahokia (above). These were the homes of the farmers who supplied the city with food. In their fields they grew corn, beans, and squash—a kind of marrow. They stored their surplus crops in pits dug in the ground outside their houses.

▲ This pottery bottle, modeled in the shape of a mother nursing her child, comes from the Cahokia area. Mississippian pottery, in the form of people and various animals, may have been copies of similar pots brought from Mexico by traders.

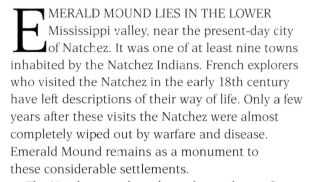

Emerald Mound

EMERALD MOUND LIES IN THE LOWER Mississippi valley, near the present-day city of Natchez. It was one of at least nine towns inhabited by the Natchez Indians. French explorers who visited the Natchez in the early 18th century have left descriptions of their way of life. Only a few years after these visits the Natchez were almost completely wiped out by warfare and disease. Emerald Mound remains as a monument to these considerable settlements.

The Natchez may have been descendants of the earlier Mound Builders. They were ruled by a powerful chief called the Great Sun. He wore elaborate feather crowns and cloaks and was carried everywhere in a litter. His subjects treated him with great respect. Anyone who displeased him was put to death. When the Great Sun died, his wife and servants were killed and buried with him.

▶ Emerald Mound is a natural hill that was flattened to make a large platform 770 ft (230 m) long and 440 ft (130 m) wide. Two earthen flat-topped pyramids were built on top. The larger one measures almost 33 ft (10 m) high.

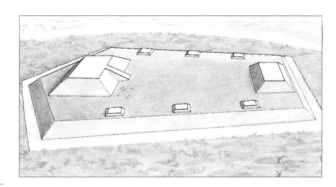

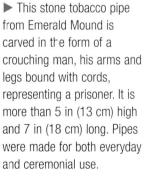

▶ This stone tobacco pipe from Emerald Mound is carved in the form of a crouching man, his arms and legs bound with cords, representing a prisoner. It is more than 5 in (13 cm) high and 7 in (18 cm) long. Pipes were made for both everyday and ceremonial use.

The Natchez chief's pipe-bearer was one of his most important servants. When the chief died, his pipe-bearer was killed and buried with him.

The Northern Iroquoians

IN WOODLANDS TO THE NORTHEAST OF the Mississippian people lived the Northern Iroquoians. By about 1000 C.E. they had spread over a wide area around the eastern Great Lakes and along the St. Lawrence river valley. When European explorers first met the Iroquoians in the 16th century, they were divided into 12 tribes (see map).

Village life

The Iroquoians were hunters, farmers, and also traders, living in villages set among their fields. In the surrounding woods the men hunted deer, bear, and caribou. They also trapped smaller animals such as rabbits and beavers. The women cultivated the fields with hoes and digging sticks. They planted the seeds and tended the young crops.

The most important crops were those known as the "three sisters"—corn, beans, and squash. After about 10 or 15 years, the soil became exhausted and the fields had to be abandoned. The men cleared another patch of forest to make more fields, and a new village was built nearby.

Early Iroquoian villages were built on the banks of streams or rivers. Later, because the people feared attack from neighboring tribes, their villages were often built on hilltops and protected by great wooden palisades arranged in three rows with watch-towers: ". . . and these they stock with stones in wartime to hurl upon the enemy, and water to put out the fire that might be laid against their palisades," wrote Gabriel Sagard, a 17th-century missionary who worked among the Huron.

Villages sometimes formed leagues for the purpose of war or trade, but there was no central government within a tribe. Each village was ruled by an elected chief with a council to advise him and help him keep order.

Longhouses

An Iroquoian village consisted of a number of longhouses, each one occupied by several related families. Longhouses were built of frameworks of wooden poles covered over with sheets of bark. They varied in size, but one housing 20 families might be 150 feet (46 m) long.

Inside the longhouse, each family had its own section, 13 feet (4 m) long, partitioned off from its neighbors. A row of fireplaces ran along the middle of the floor, one for every two families. Gaps were left open in the roof to allow the smoke to escape. Food and firewood were stored at one end of the house,

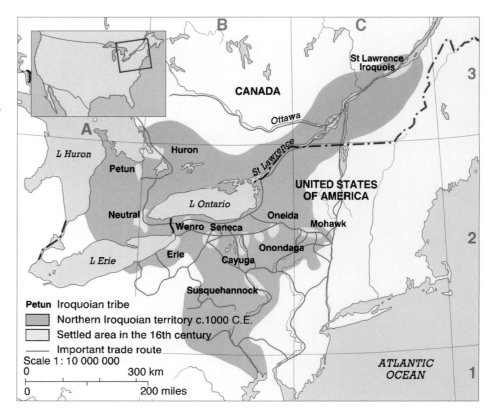

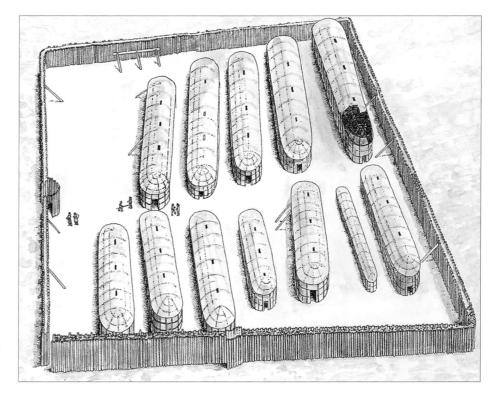

▲ The 12 tribes of Northern Iroquoians lived around the eastern Great Lakes and along the St. Lawrence valley.

▼ The Mohawk village of Caughnawaga, built about 1690. Earlier villages were larger, with perhaps 50 longhouses occupied by as many as 2,000 people. This site, west of the Hudson River, is a rare preserved Iroquois village.

▼ Iroquoian clothing was made from skins and furs. In warm weather, men, their bodies painted and tattooed, wore only a deerskin breechcloth and moccasins. In winter they wore a cloak, long sleeves, and leggings. This male carries a carved wooden club with a heavy rounded end.

▼ Deer hunting was often a joint activity. Several hundred hunters might band together to drive the deer into a specially built enclosure. The animals were then killed with spears.

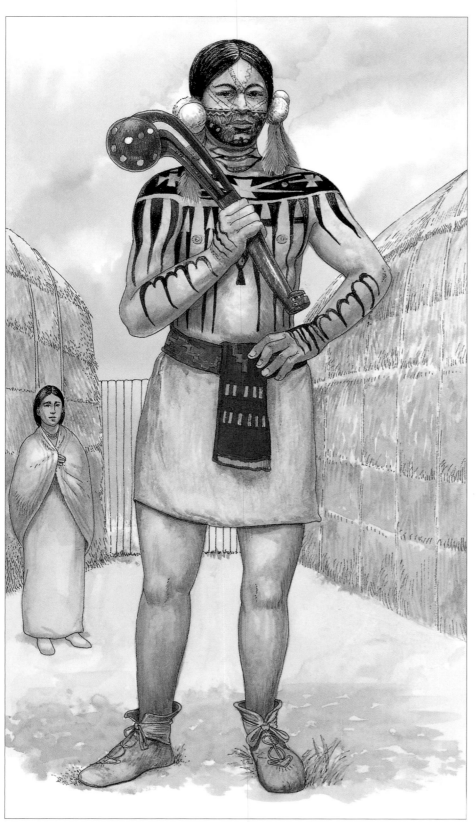

and in the center there were racks where people kept their belongings—their clothes, hunting weapons, farming tools, baskets, cooking pots and utensils, and birchbark bowls for serving food. Around the walls were low wooden benches covered with skins for sitting or sleeping. In winter, people slept underneath the benches for greater warmth.

The fur trade

As traders, the Iroquoians traveled great distances over land on foot or along the rivers by bark canoe. The Huron, for example, traded corn, tobacco, and fishing nets to neighboring tribes, receiving meat and furs in return.

After the arrival of French and English traders in the Eastern Woodlands in the 16th century, the fur trade became very important. In exchange for furs, the traders supplied the Iroquoians with European goods such as beads, cloth, metal tools, and guns.

The growth of the fur trade caused fighting to break out among the Iroquoians as different tribes tried to control the trade routes. Many people were killed in these wars, and many more died of European diseases such as smallpox.

As a result, the Iroquoian population declined so much that when French and English colonists arrived in the Woodlands in the early 17th century, they found vast areas that were no longer inhabited. The Iroquoian federation of six tribes, often known as the Iroquois, mostly sided with the British in their 18th-century wars against the French and Americans.

The Great Plains

THE GREAT PLAINS STRETCH RIGHT ACROSS central North America from the Mississippi River to the Rocky Mountains. In the prehistoric period, up to about 1500 C.E., most Plains Indians were farmers, living in villages in the eastern prairies. Only a few nomadic buffalo hunters lived in the High Plains to the west (see map).

The eastern prairies

Along the upper Mississippi valley and on the eastern prairies people began settling down and cultivating at least a few plants from 500 B.C.E.

By about 1000 C.E. farming villages were present on terraces or bluffs along the valley, and some of the ancestors of these people may have come from farther east. Crops were grown in the flood plain below the villages, the most important being corn, beans, and squash.

People probably left their villages once or twice a year to go on long hunting trips. Large quantities of buffalo bones have been found at village sites. The main farming tool was a hoe made from a buffalo shoulder bone lashed to a wooden handle.

◄ Typical Great Plains landscape, showing a "buffalo jump." Until Europeans brought horses to America, Native Americans hunted buffalo and other game on foot. Often hunters banded together to stampede a herd over a cliff, like the one shown here.

The American artist, Paul Kane, reported in the 1840s that ". . . there are thousands of them [buffalo] killed annually . . . but not one in 20 is used in any way by the Indians so that thousands are left to rot where they fall."

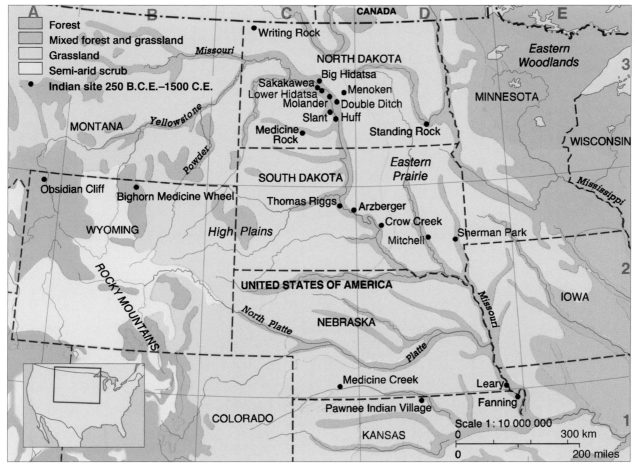

◄ Most of the Plains Indians were farmers before the Europeans arrived. They grew corn and other crops along the river valleys of the eastern Plains. Here the soil was light and easily worked with Indian farming tools such as hoes and digging sticks. The richer, heavier soil of the prairies was not cultivated until the arrival of European plows and draft animals. In the western or High Plains there were only a few nomadic Indians, who were hunters all the year around.

The High Plains

In the western Plains, the climate was too dry for farming. The 16th-century Spanish explorer Francisco de Coronado (see page 12) wrote scathingly of the Plains Indians whom he met that "they do not plant anything and do not have any houses except of skin and sticks and they wander around with the cows."

These were the nomadic hunters who lived in skin tents and followed the buffalo herds on foot. They had few possessions, since everything had to be carried on their backs or by their dogs. Dogs were trained to pull a *travois* (a type of sled).

▲ A Pawnee village in the Great Plains in Nebraska, photographed in 1871. Bundles of tipi poles are stacked against the entrance passage to the earth lodge. Pawnee families lived in tipis when they went on their long summer hunting trips.

▶ From the 15th century Plains farmers lived in large dome-shaped earth lodges. Like their earlier houses, these were built of wood covered with turf and earth. Entry was through a covered passage. Inside, there was a central fireplace with a smoke hole in the roof above. Raised wooden platforms running along the wall were used as benches or beds.

Before the reintroduction of the horse, Prairie tribes used dogs for hunting, pulling *travois* (sleds), and carrying lightweight loads.

Life on the Plains

PLAINS INDIANS ARE USUALLY DEPICTED as mounted warriors wearing fringed buckskin and feathered headdresses. But this way of life lasted only a short time—less than 100 years. The reason that it existed at all was because of the horse. This lifestyle ended by about the 1880s with the European expansion—by horse—across the Plains.

Horses had once lived wild in America, but they died out about 10,000 years ago. Domesticated horses were brought to America by 16th-century Spanish settlers. At first the Spaniards refused to sell horses to the Indians, but the Indians got hold of them by raiding Spanish ranches or capturing strays. By about 1800 most Plains tribes had managed to obtain at least a few horses. Horses changed their way of life.

With horses the Indians were able to travel farther and faster than ever before. Buffalo hunting became an easier and more attractive form of livelihood. More people moved out into the Plains to become nomadic hunters. These included people such as the Lakota (Sioux), Cheyenne, and Arapaho who had been farmers, and the Cree who had been hunters and trappers in the Eastern Woodlands.

Tribes, tipis, and ceremonies

During the fall and winter the Plains tribes split up into small bands, each with its own chief. In spring the bands left the shelter of their winter quarters and moved out onto the Plains. In summer they all came together, pitching their cone-shaped tents, or tipis, in one great camp circle.

The Plains tipi was made of buffalo skin stretched over a framework of wooden poles. Inside, a lining of more skins kept out the drafts. Smoke from the central fireplace escaped through an opening at the top that could be opened or closed according to the direction of the wind. The tipi was, in fact, very well designed for life on the Plains. It was warm in winter and cool in summer, and it was waterproof. Most important of all, it could be quickly dismantled and packed up when it was time to move camp.

Summer was the time for organizing communal activities and for holding tribal councils and ceremonies. The most important ceremony held at this time was the annual Sun Dance. This was when people joined together to offer prayers and thanks for supernatural help in times of trouble. The ceremony lasted for several days and it was called the Sun Dance because many of those taking part gazed at the sky as they offered their prayers.

Hunting buffalo

The buffalo gave the Plains Indians almost everything they needed. The meat was eaten fresh or dried and stored in bags. The skins, cleaned and dressed, were made into clothing, bedding, tipi covers, bags, and riding tackle. Tools were made from the bones, ropes from the hair, thread from the sinews, and cups and spoons from the horns.

Ways of hunting varied with the seasons and the movements of the buffalo. In winter men hunted in small groups, on foot if the snow was deep. Then they might use the age-old method of surrounding a herd and driving it into a corral or over a cliff.

When the whole tribe gathered for the summer camp, hundreds of mounted hunters joined together to pursue the buffalo on the open Plains. The hunters approached downwind of the buffalo to conceal their scent from the herd. The shaman, or medicine man, invoked the spirits' aid for a successful hunt. The hunters made their kills on horseback, using lances or bows and arrows.

◄ Mato-Topé, a Mandan chief, painted in 1832. His shirt decorations show that he has scalped many enemies (cut the skin and hair from the top of the head). The wooden knife records his killing of a Cheyenne chief in hand-to-hand combat. Mato-Topé, along with most of his tribe, died of smallpox in 1837.

◀ In each tribe there were several men's societies. Their duties included protecting the camp or village and organizing hunting and war parties. Each society had its own dances that it performed on special occasions. The Mandan Bull Society, shown here in a painting, danced in spring to lure the buffalo herds closer to the village.

▼ A buffalo hunt, pictured by American painter George Catlin in the 1830s. Mounted hunters surround a buffalo herd, shooting them down as they mill about in confusion. Fifty years later the buffalo had gone and the Indians were confined to reservations. Painters like Catlin captured this way of life before it vanished forever.

The Far West

WEST OF THE GREAT PLAINS, BETWEEN the Rocky Mountains and the Sierra Nevada, lies a vast wilderness of desert and mountain. Here Native American farming methods were not possible. Much of the area was too dry and desolate to support people.

The Great Basin

The southern part of the region is known as the Great Basin. Only small scattered bands of hunters and gatherers lived here. The women foraged among the sparse grass and scrubby bushes for seeds and nuts, which they ground into flour and made into porridge or bread. Large game such as deer were scarce, but the men hunted rabbits, birds, lizards, and rats, as well as small insects such as grasshoppers and caterpillars.

Their search for food kept them constantly on the move. In summer they lived in flimsy brush shelters on the banks of shallow lakes and streams. During the winter they camped in rock shelters or caves in the mountains. At each campsite they left supplies of flour and dried fruit and meat in storage pits ready for their next visit.

The Plateau

To the north of the Great Basin, around the headwaters of the Columbia and Fraser Rivers, is the Plateau, an area of grassland and mountains. The Plateau Indians also gathered wild fruit and plants for food. The bulb of the camass lily, closely related to the hyacinth, was one of their most important sources of food.

There was a greater variety of wildlife here than in the Great Basin. The rivers teemed with fish,

---

Life in the West 1000 B.C.E.–1800 C.E.

In the desert basin Seeds and nuts (especially pine nuts) gathered. Digging sticks used to collect roots. Bows and arrows for hunting deer; nets and traps for catching small game. Clothing from skins and plant fibers; cloaks and blankets of twisted strips of rabbit fur.
On the plateau Fish (especially salmon) caught in rivers with spears, nets, traps, and weirs. Bows and arrows for hunting. Baskets for carrying, storing, and cooking. Clothing from skins, fur, and plant fibers.

California 500–1800 C.E.
Seeds and nuts (especially acorns) ground into flour using mortars and pestles. Shellfish caught, fishing with spears and bone and shellfish hooks along the coast. Bows and arrows for hunting. Round dome-shaped houses with thatched roofs.

▶ The Pomo Indians of California made baskets like this as gifts and ceremonial offerings. They decorated the surfaces with feathers and beads.

▼ Prehistoric sites in California are located mainly on the coast and along rivers.

especially salmon. Deer, antelope, and mountain sheep were hunted in the northern forests and mountains. Because food was easier to find, the Indians were able to lead a more settled way of life. For part of the year they lived in villages of "earth lodges." In summer they moved to camps at the fishing grounds.

California

Beyond the Sierra Nevada, in what is now California, the land was rich in natural resources. The valleys were full of game, and the hills were covered with acorn-bearing oaks. Acorns, the staple diet of the

▼ Acorns, the main food of the Californian Indians, were poisonous if not treated carefully. They were first pounded into flour, which was put in a basket and rinsed to remove the harmful acids. The Indians made shelters from brushwood, as here.

▶ The Fremont people lived in Utah between 400 and 1300 C.E. Little is known about them, but clay figurines like this have been found at their sites.

Californian Indians, were pounded into flour in a mortar and boiled with hot stones to make a mushy porridge. The rivers and sea provided many kinds of fish, which the Indians caught with hooks and spears. They pried shellfish from the rocks and hunted seals, dolphins, porpoises, and whales from their canoes.

The rich vegetation made food gathering easier and also provided the women with materials for making mats and baskets. Baskets had many uses. Some were for collecting and storing food. Others were so finely woven that they could hold water, even without being waterproofed with pitch, and these were used for cooking. Baskets made as gifts or for ceremonies were especially beautiful, often covered entirely with brilliantly colored feathers and hung with clamshell beads. Shell beads and feathers were also made into items of jewelry. Everyday clothing was scanty, consisting of breechcloths for men and skirts for women, though rabbit-skin robes were put on in colder weather. Body paint and elaborate feather cloaks and headdresses were worn at special ceremonies.

The Southwest

THE SOUTHWEST COVERS THE MODERN states of Arizona and New Mexico, together with southern Utah and Colorado as well as part of northern Mexico. Although much of the area is desert, there is enough rainfall for farming in some parts at least. Corn has been grown in the region since before 1000 B.C.E. Later crops include beans, squash, and cotton.

The prehistoric Southwest was home to several groups of farmers, for example, the Hohokam, the Mogollon, and the Anasazi.

The Hohokam

The Hohokam people settled in the valleys of the Salt and Gila Rivers in southern Arizona. They seem to have had many links with Mexico.

Hohokam farmers built a network of canals to draw river water onto the fertile flood plain where they planted their crops. This system of irrigation enabled the Hohokam to grow two crops a year, one in spring when the river swelled with melting snow and the other in late summer when heavy rain fell.

Their early houses, built of wattle and daub, were set in shallow pits dug in the desert sand. Later they built larger houses of adobe (sun-dried mud-brick) entirely above ground. The Great House at Casa Grande is four stories high and has massive adobe walls that are more than 3 feet (1 m) thick.

The Mogollon

The Mogollon people lived in the mountainous region stretching from southern New Mexico and Arizona into northern Mexico. Like the Hohokam, the Mogollon at first lived in pit houses. From about 1000 C.E. they too began to build large multistory

▶ This cliff dwelling in central Arizona was built about 1200 C.E. by Sinagua farmers in the Verde valley. It was named Montezuma Castle by early Spanish explorers who thought it had been built by Aztecs from Mexico.

▶ The Hohokam town of Snaketown flourished between 200 and 1200 C.E. The inhabitants dug a system of irrigation canals which carried water from the Gila River to their fields. This allowed them to grow two crops a year instead of only one. In this scene, children play a string game and a man and woman make spear tips beside a stone palette that may have been coated with water and used as a mirror.

houses of stone and adobe, which often contained 100 or more rooms.

These later villages included "kivas," round underground rooms where the men of the village held meetings and performed religious ceremonies.

The Anasazi

The Anasazi were centered on the "Four Corners" area, where the modern boundaries of Arizona, New Mexico, Colorado, and Utah meet. By 700 C.E. most of the Anasazi had abandoned their earlier pit dwellings in favor of multiroomed houses built of stone and adobe.

In Chaco Canyon in northern New Mexico the Anasazi built huge planned towns such as Pueblo Bonito and Chetro Ketl. Here hundreds of rooms arranged on several levels housed many hundreds of people.

North of Chaco Canyon at Mesa Verde (Spanish for "green table"), villages were at first built on top of the cliffs. But in about 1100, for reasons that are not fully understood, nearly all the villages moved to more sheltered sites in the cliff face. These are the very spectacular cliff dwellings for which the Southwest is now famous (see pages 42–45).

Drought and abandonment

By 1300 C.E. farming people on the Colorado Plateau had abandoned their villages. Persistent drought, crop failures, together with competition from newly arrived hunter-gatherer groups, are the most likely explanations for this. Many people relocated farther south to escape the unfavorable conditions.

Today their descendants continue to live in Southwestern villages, and many still build terraced houses several stories high. The Pima and Papago Indians are probably descended from the Hohokam, the Zuni from the Mogollon, and the Hopi from the Anasazi. The Zuni and Hopi belong to the group now known as Pueblo.

Mimbres Pottery

DURING THE 11TH CENTURY THE PEOPLE of the Mimbres valley in southwestern New Mexico began to decorate their pottery in a new and interesting way, with a liveliness of design and quality of painting not seen before. Probably, as in modern New Mexico, pots were made and decorated by the women of each village.

Most Mimbres pottery takes the form of shallow bowls painted inside with designs in black and white or in shades of orange and red. Some are painted

◀ (Above) A bowl found in the grave of a young woman who died in about 1100. The design is a clever combination of a bird and a human head.

◀ (Below) This bowl, like the one above, has a "killing hole" in its base. Here a man seems to be whirling a bull roarer—a flat piece of wood or bone attached to a length of cord. When whirled quickly, it makes a loud roaring noise. It may have been used in ceremonies to call up spirits, or to bring game or rain.

▼ Mimbres designs often depict strange beings from myth or legend. This figure seems to be part man, part deer, and part bat. It may represent a costumed dancer. In San Juan Pueblo in northern New Mexico, dancers wearing antlers still perform a Deer Dance to ensure enough game for the coming year.

with geometric patterns such as triangles and zigzags. Others have designs that show humans and animals, including birds and insects. These designs tell us a good deal about the way of life of the people who painted them. They show, for example, deer, mountain sheep, and rabbits, which the Mimbres people hunted for food.

Sometimes the painting depicts the sort of clothing and jewelry worn. Women, for example, are often shown wearing sandals and a blanket with a fringed sash hanging down behind.

▼ Although the bowls themselves were often poorly made, Mimbres potters—believed to be only the women—took great care with their decoration. They mixed their paints from plants, crushed rocks, and earth. Brushes were made from feathers, twigs, and stems that were chewed until the ends became soft and flexible. The bowls were not fired in a kiln. Instead, firewood was heaped around them and they were baked in a slow-burning bonfire.

Underfloor burials

Mimbres pottery is often found in burials. The Mimbres people buried their dead under the floors of their houses, even when they went on living above. People were usually buried with various grave offerings, including at least one painted bowl with a punctured base.

Freeing the potter's spirit

Before the bowls were placed in the grave they were ceremonially "killed." This means that each bowl had a hole punched through the bottom of it, using some kind of sharp instrument.

It is possible that this was done in an attempt to release the spirit or soul of the bowl's maker, since this was thought to be a part of the bowl.

Mesa Verde

MESAS—STEEP-SIDED HILLS WITH FLAT tops—are typical features of the Southwestern landscape. Mesa Verde is now a national park in Colorado. During the 12th century the Anasazi people built huge terraced houses in the shelter of the mesa's overhanging cliffs. These cliff dwellings were, in fact, large villages housing hundreds of people. Their design suggests they were built for defense against raids by other groups. There are no ground-floor doors or windows. Instead, ladders provided access to the dwellings.

The people of Mesa Verde were farmers. Traces of their fields and irrigation terraces can still be seen on the flat top of the mesa. Most of the cliff dwellings in Mesa Verde were abandoned early in the 14th century. As elsewhere in the Southwest, this was a result of drought, crop failure, and the arrival of new groups, preceded by increasingly violent competition over areas of land among the Anasazi communities themselves.

Cliff Palace

Of the many ruins in Mesa Verde National Park, the largest and most famous is Cliff Palace. It contains more than 400 rooms and its massive walls are four stories high in places. It was not, in fact, a palace, although its many rooms and stone towers perhaps give it the appearance of one.

The rooms were small, often oddly shaped, and had low ceilings. While some of the rooms had windows and doors, others seem to have been entered through the roof, most likely by a ladder. Some rooms were living quarters, with one family in each room. Others were used for storage—probably for food supplies and stocks of seed corn. Yet other rooms may have been for communal milling, in which the women ground the corn.

There are as many as 23 kivas (see page 39) at Cliff Palace. This is a large number, and some archaeologists have suggested that Cliff Palace may have been a religious center for all the people of Mesa Verde.

The Cliff Palace towers would have served well as fortress homes, but it is also possible that they were used as observatories for following the position of the sun to calculate the best times for planting and harvesting crops.

Canyon de Chelly

ANYON DE CHELLY IS A NATIONAL monument in northeastern Arizona. The area is one of mountain ranges cut by steep-sided canyons more than 650 feet (200 m) deep. Here, as at Mesa Verde, 12th-century Anasazi farmers built their tall cliff houses in the shelter of the enormous canyon walls. They cut climbing holes for their hands and feet in the sheer face of the cliff, to enable them to climb to the top of the canyon.

The Anasazi chose to live here because the canyon floor provided the best farming land in the area. They built their houses in order to have a clear outlook over their fields. There are about 150 cliff dwellings along the 18-mile (30-km) length of Canyon de Chelly. They are built of sandstone blocks cut from the canyon walls. Most are relatively small and would have housed perhaps no more than 30 or 40 people at any one time.

As well as living accommodation, the cliff dwellings also include storage rooms and kivas (underground meeting rooms). Although protected by the overhanging cliffs, most houses faced south and remained open to the sun. The interiors of the houses were cool in summer and warm in winter.

◀ The ruins of Cliff Palace, seen in winter from the cliff above. Far from being the palace of a ruler, it was, in fact, home to hundreds of Anasazi farmers and their families. Each family occupied one small room.

The round buildings at the front are kivas (underground meeting rooms), now roofless. When complete, their roofs formed open courtyards for the buildings behind.

▶ The White House, the remains of an Anasazi cliff dwelling, appears almost overwhelmed by the massive walls of Canyon de Chelly. The White House ruin is, in fact, in two parts. The smaller, upper part is shown here, while 30 ft (9 m) below, another cluster of about 45 rooms lies on the floor of the canyon, tucked against the cliff face. These dwellings were not designed to any fixed plan. Their shape depended on that of the caves and niches that sheltered them.

Chaco Canyon

CHACO CANYON LIES IN AN ISOLATED PART of northwestern New Mexico, about 95 miles (153 km) south of Mesa Verde. Between 900 and 1100 C.E. the Anasazi built 12 huge planned towns along the canyon. In these towns hundreds of people lived in multistory blocks of rooms built of stone and adobe.

The towns were linked to each other and to the outside world by a wide network of roads. Traders

▼ Even in its ruined state, Pueblo Bonito is impressive. It was called the biggest apartment block in the world until a larger one was built in New York in 1882. Living rooms and kivas (meeting rooms) can be seen ranged around the curving rear wall.

As the building grew, the earliest rooms at the back were completely enclosed. Lacking windows and with entry only through the roof, they were probably used for storage. Living rooms were large, with plastered walls. Few of them seem to have had fireplaces, so cooking was probably done outside on the terraces.

Several very large kivas, or meeting rooms (see page 39), were sunk into the central plaza, and the

came, bringing goods from distant places, such as shells from the Pacific coast and copper bells and brightly feathered birds from Mexico. Other goods would have flowed back along these roads, for the towns were full of skilled craftsmen and women— potters, weavers, makers of fine baskets and feather cloaks, and carvers of shell, turquoise, and jet.

Pueblo Bonito

Pueblo Bonito is the largest and also the most spectacular of the Chaco Canyon settlements. Early Spanish explorers were so impressed by its appearance that they gave it its present name— Spanish for "pretty village."

The town faces south toward the Chaco River, with its curving rear wall tucked against the cliffs of the canyon. Its 800 rooms rise in terraces around the central plaza like a vast amphitheater. The roofs of the lower tiers provided open terraces for the rooms above, rising at least four stories above ground level.

▶ Pueblo Bonito saw its heyday in the 12th century, but despite its size it may have housed as few as 100 people. The settlement is in the shape of a huge D, with its round back to the canyon wall. Entrance was by ladder. Archaeologists now think that many fewer people lived here than was once believed. Instead of being mostly residential, Pueblo Bonito may have served primarily as a sacred site, a place of pilgrimage that drew visitors from a wide area. Its many kivas and evidence of long-distance contacts support this interpretation.

site also has many burials and caches of ritual objects, all of which suggests that it was the focus of much religious activity.

Fear of attack

Pueblo Bonito seems to have been solidly built for defense. At the front there were no windows on the lowest level, and there were none in the curving side at all. The original single gateway was first narrowed

▶ Chaco Canyon potters made jugs, bowls, and ladles with decorative geometric designs. Women made the pottery by hand, coiling thin rolls of clay on top of one another. The potter's wheel was a technology unknown in the Americas at this time.

and finally blocked up completely. Entry to the town was only by means of ladders that could be pulled up by those inside.

It is not clear what sort of attack the inhabitants feared. The Apache and Navajo raiders who ravaged the *pueblos* (villages) in later centuries had yet to make their appearance in the Southwest.

Abandonment of the towns

The Chaco towns, like Anasazi settlements elsewhere, were dependent on agriculture. Farmers irrigated their crops by collecting rainwater and channeling it to their fields.

This, however, was not enough to save them from the droughts that affected the Southwest during the last quarter of the 13th century. Crops failed and the whole Chaco Canyon way of life began to collapse. By the early 14th century, the inhabitants had moved away to other areas and these once thriving centers were left deserted.

Chaco Canyon is remarkable for its buildings, roads, dams, and mounds—all of which indicate its significance as a ceremonial and trade center. Until the 19th century and the advent of the first skyscrapers, Pueblo Bonito was the largest human-made housing structure in North America. Around the canyon were numerous "outlier" towns, many of which are as yet unstudied.

Hopi Ritual Drama

THE HOPI STILL LIVE IN EIGHT VILLAGES, OR pueblos, perched on three mesas in northern Arizona. Today they number around 7,000. Like their Anasazi ancestors who inhabited this area over 1,000 years ago, they are farmers. And in much the same way as the Anasazi did, the Hopi continue to plant their crops of corn, beans, and squash.

Because the Hopi live in a dry, semidesert area where farming is difficult, they give great importance to performing complicated rituals that are designed to bring rain and produce good harvests. The average Hopi man probably spends almost half his time either preparing for or taking part in dances and ceremonies.

Seasonal ceremonies and dancing

The annual round of ceremonies begins in November with Wuwuchim, which celebrates the creation of the world. The various religious societies hold their ceremonies in the kivas.

From December through July the "kachinas" (see below) dance and sing in the plaza to bring good fortune to the village. They are supernatural beings who are impersonated by masked dancers. All the parts, even those of female kachinas, are taken by men.

In mid-August the Flute or Snake societies perform ceremonies to bring rain. Finally, in September and October, the women's societies dance to welcome the harvest.

The kachinas

The kachinas are very important to the Hopi. There are more than 300 of them, all different. They can be recognized by their painted masks and brightly colored costumes. Some are the spirits of tribal ancestors. Others are animal spirits or natural forces, such as rain, wind, cloud, and thunder.

In February the kachinas visit Hopi villages for Powamu, the bean-planting ceremony. Led by the Kachina Mother, they enter the village at dawn. They run among the spectators, handing out gifts and receiving food in return. The clown kachinas entertain the crowd with their acrobatic skills, jokes, and games. The Niman ceremony in July marks the kachinas' return to Kachina Village, their distant mythical home in the mountains. They will not be seen again until December when they return to celebrate the winter solstice.

Children were encouraged to learn kachina dances by copying them. Their play-acting was seen by American archaeologist, J. Fewkes, who described them as follows:

"About 15 boys and girls, no more than 15 years of age, took part, each dressed in a ceremonial kilt and blanket; their bodies were painted and feathers were tied in their hair . . . and they danced and sang as do their elders. . . . Some of the children were carried into the kivas in the arms of their fathers to prevent them from slipping from the ladders." (at Walpi Pueblo, 1900)

▼ Ogre kachinas visit Hopi villages in February for the bean-planting ceremony. They threaten to carry off naughty children unless they are given presents of meat and cornmeal.

▶ Wooden dolls, carved and painted to represent kachinas, are given to Hopi children so that they can learn more about the seasonal ceremonies in which the kachinas appear.

► Two clown kachinas photographed at the bean-planting ceremony at a Hopi village in 1893. In the background stand Kachina Mother and an ogre kachina. (Taking photographs at any Hopi ceremonies was forbidden in 1911.)

▼ Unmarried girls, in their cotton mantles, and other villagers gather to watch and listen to the all-male Flute Society dancing and singing in the plaza. Every other year in August Flute and Snake society members perform ceremonies to bring rain clouds.

Northwest Coast

THE PACIFIC COAST BETWEEN SOUTHERN Alaska and northern California is a rugged strip of land with many small islands, deep inlets, and narrow beaches. In many places high mountains rise abruptly from the shore and dense forests of spruce, cedar, and fir grow all the way up to the water's edge.

Living off the sea and forests

The sea, rivers, and forests gave the Native Americans almost everything they needed. As well as abundant supplies of fish and shellfish, there were several kinds of whales, seals, sea lions, and porpoises. The forest provided raw materials for making houses, canoes, weapons, tools, boxes, and bowls. Baskets, mats, and even clothing were woven from strips of bark.

Ancient settlements and houses

Hunters and fishermen first inhabited this region 10,000 years ago. About 1000 B.C.E. the way of life typical of the Northwest Coast began to appear. It was a way of life that lasted until the 19th century. Like their 19th-century descendants—the Kwakiutl, Haida, Tsimshian, Tlingit, and others—prehistoric Native Americans lived for most of the year in villages along the coast. Although they sometimes went inland to gather berries or to hunt deer and bears, they were first and foremost fishermen and hunters of sea mammals.

Villages consisted of large rectangular houses, built of wooden planks. Each house was occupied by several related families, numbering perhaps 30 or 40 people in all. Every family had its own living area in the house, separated from that of all its neighbors by wooden screens or woven mats.

Carving in wood—totem poles

Woodworking was an important industry, and Native American craftsmen used a variety of specialized tools. Hammers, adzes, chisels, awls, and drills were made of stone, bone, and shell before the Native Americans obtained metal from traders and European settlers. Unfortunately, wood decays quickly in the damp Northwest Coast climate. Most surviving woodcarvings therefore date only from the 19th century or later.

Perhaps the best known wood carvings are totem poles. These were made for a variety of reasons. Some displayed the emblems of the families who owned them, rather like coats of arms. Some were

▶ A mask worn by a Kwakiutl dancer in the role of Bowkus, a wild being who lured the spirits of drowned people to his home in the woods.

▼ High mountains separated the rocky Pacific coast from the interior. Here a warm, wet climate has produced a land rich in natural resources.

put up to commemorate important events or as memorials to the dead. Others were house posts built on the fronts of houses, with doorways cut in their bases.

Masked dancers and potlatches

Carved and painted wooden masks were (and still are) used in dances and ceremonies. Many were worn in dances that acted out legends of ancestors and family origins. Performances were often very dramatic. Masked dancers might sometimes appear suddenly through trap doors or swing through the air on ropes to give the illusion of flying.

The masks usually depicted supernatural beings with whom ancestral heroes had come into contact. These beings often appeared in the form of animals or birds. When a dancer put on a mask, he took on the personality of the spirit that it represented.

There were many different types of masks. Among the most elaborate were those known as "transformation" masks. By pulling hidden strings, the wearer of this kind of mask could open it up to reveal another, quite different mask within. Some of these masks were so heavy that the dancer had to wear a special harness strapped to his body.

People of high social status gave feasts, known as potlatches—traditionally featuring seal meat or salmon—during which they distributed gifts. Gift-giving reaffirmed the rank of both the donor and the recipient.

▲ Although this wood Bella Coola mask appears to be a human face, the style indicates an animal spirit.

◄ A totem pole put up to make fun of a white trader who cheated Indians. His face, carved at the pole's top, could be jeered at.

▼ Many masks were worn in dances that acted out myths. These told of ancestral heroes and their adventures with supernatural beings, who took the form of animals or monsters. The wearer of this Nootka bird mask could make it seem more realistic by opening and closing its beak.

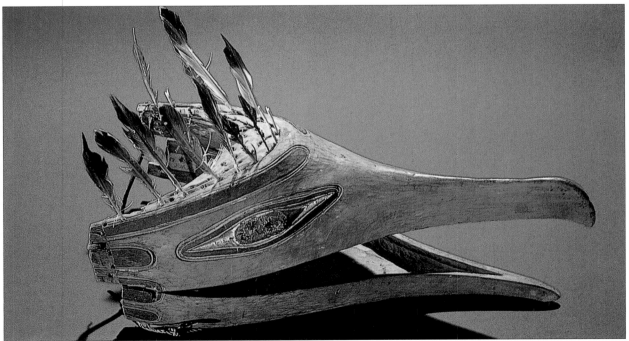

Part Two

The History
of Latin America

▲ A stylized person on a painted bowl from Panama. The design shows stronger influences from South America than from North America.

▶ A view of Machu Picchu in Peru, showing its complex structure, varied stonework, and dramatic setting.

Latin America: Land and Climate

LATIN AMERICA CONSISTS OF THOSE AREAS where Spanish or Portuguese (two languages that are derived from Latin) are spoken. The areas are Mexico, the countries of Central and South America, and the Spanish-speaking Caribbean islands (see map on page 9).

Stretching southward from the United States border to the cold and stormy waters of the south Atlantic, Latin America has enormous variations in both climate and landscape.

Mexico and Central America

Much of Central America has a tropical or sub-tropical climate, although in the north and in Mexico there are deserts and dry grasslands. Hurricanes sweeping in from the Atlantic Ocean often batter the coastline. In the southern lowlands, areas of swamp and tropical forest result from a heavy seasonal rainfall.

South America

Amazonia, the name given to the great Amazon River basin, covers more than 2,800,000 square miles (4,500,000 sq. km)—almost the size of Australia. It is a vast area of rain forest (*selvas*), the home of scattered Native American groups.

They lived by clearing small patches of forest to grow crops before moving on. They had little impact on the forest, which soon recovered. Now, however, vast areas are being cleared for commercial purposes, and unless we take action the rain forest will be destroyed forever.

North and south of the rain forest there are drier tropical areas of grassland called *llanos*, or *campos*. Farther south lie the hot dry scrubland of the Gran Chaco and the rolling grasslands known as the *pampas*. To the south, from Patagonia, the land becomes increasingly cold and bleak. Cape Horn, at the tip of Tierra del Fuego, is famous for its storms.

▼ Circular terraced slopes in the southern highlands of Peru show how people have changed the landscape to suit their needs. In the mountains there are few broad valleys in which crops can be grown, but Inca farmers created flat fields by cutting these steplike terraces down the steep hillsides. The terraces are supported by stone walls, and stone steps led from one level to the next. Drainage channels carry water from terraces on the upper slopes to those many feet lower down.

► The great range of natural vegetation in Latin America is shown on this map. For example, in the hot and steamy Amazon jungle—the world's greatest rain forest—the rainfall averages 60 to 100 inches (150–250 cm) each year. By contrast, the Atacama Desert, along the coasts of Peru and northern Chile, receives almost no rain.

The Amazon River, together with its great network of tributaries, meanders across much of Brazil and eight other countries. The Amazonian rain forest is now being lost at a rate of 2 percent—the size of Belgium—each year.

Gulf of Mexico

Sierra Madre Occidental
Sierra Madre Oriental
Yucatán
Isthmus of Tehuantepec

Cuba
Greater Antilles
Jamaica
Hispaniola
Lesser Antilles

Caribbean Sea

Lake Nicaragua

Galápagos Is

Orinoco
Llanos
GUIANA HIGHLANDS

Japurá
Ucayali
Selvas
Amazon
Madeira
Araguaia

A N D E S
Lake Titicaca
Altiplano
Atacama Desert

PACIFIC OCEAN

Gran Chaco
Paraguay
Paraná
BRAZILIAN HIGHLANDS

ATLANTIC OCEAN

Paraná

A N D E S
Pampas
Colorado

Patagonia

Tierra del Fuego
Cape Horn

Mountain vegetation
Mixed forest
Temperate and subtropical forest
Tropical rainforest
Grassland
Semidesert and scrub
Desert

Equatorial scale 1 : 62 000 000

◄ The area around Lake Titicaca, at some 13,200 feet (4,000 m) above sea level, is bleak and often very cold. Yet people have lived here for more than 10,000 years. In sheltered areas, corn and cotton have been grown, and around the lake shores people fished and hunted waterbirds and deer.

Mesoamerica After the Ice Age

BY MESOAMERICA WE MEAN THE PARTS of Mexico and Central America that were civilized before the Spanish Conquest. In Mesoamerica, as elsewhere, the ending of the Ice Age brought changes in the climate and landscape, at least in the highlands of central and southern Mexico. As the climate became drier and warmer, grasslands turned into deserts. The herds of large grazing animals, such as mammoth, mastodon, horse, and giant bison, disappeared, leaving smaller game such as rabbit and deer, for people to hunt. The Native Americans learned to adapt to changes in their environment by developing new hunting methods and tools, especially those for grinding seeds and nuts.

In fact, hunting may not have been particularly important in this area. People may have concentrated as much, if not more, on collecting wild plants for food. Mesoamerica has always been rich in plant food. Even the desert areas produce edible plants such as mesquite, cactus, and agave, which people could readily gather.

Archaic farming

The change from gathering plants to growing them for food took place over several thousand years. The period during which this change took place is called the Archaic period. It is not clear exactly how the change came about. To save time and effort, people may have decided to plant extra supplies of their favorite food where they could be sure of finding it.

The Archaic period c.8000–2000 B.C.E.

c.8000 B.C.E. Nomadic hunters grew crops such as squash and bottle gourds near campsites.

c.4300 B.C.E. Corn grown in valley of Oaxaca.

c.3000 B.C.E. Villages of pithouses (partly underground dwellings, with wattle and daub sides) formed.

c.2300 B.C.E. People begin to make pottery.

The Formative period c.2000 B.C.E.–1 C.E. (central Mexico) and c.2000 B.C.E.–290 C.E. (Maya highlands)

c.1200 B.C.E. Rise of Olmec civilization.

c.400 B.C.E. Zapotec city of Monte Albán founded.

c.150 C.E. Rise of the city of Teotihuacán.

▼ Genetic studies suggest that the Balsas valley may have been where corn was first grown. The earliest evidence for it comes from dry caves in Oaxaca and Tehuacán.

The farming villages that appeared during the Formative period (from around 2000 B.C.E.) tended to flourish in more humid areas such as the Pacific and Gulf coasts, the Maya lowlands, and the fertile highland valleys of Oaxaca and valley of Mexico. There were also elaborate ceremonial centers from this time. Improved strains of corn and other crops were grown in several areas.

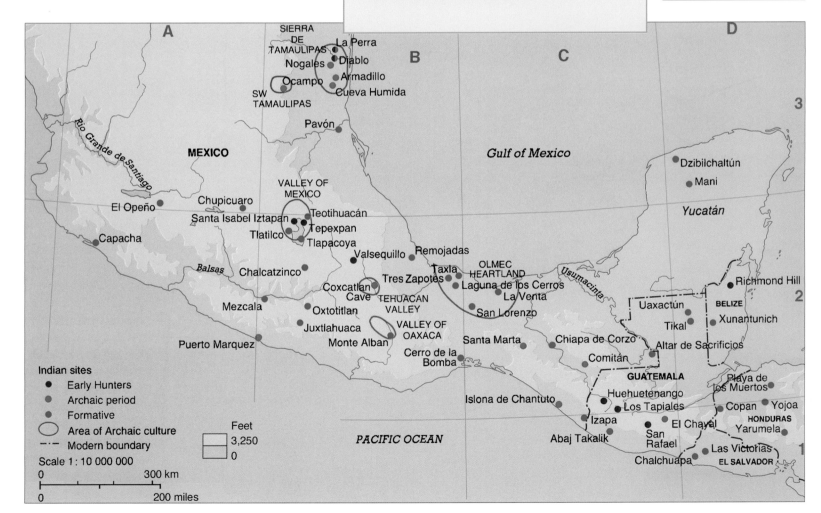

Indian sites
- Early Hunters
- Archaic period
- Formative
- ⬭ Area of Archaic culture
- Modern boundary

Feet
3,250
0

Scale 1 : 10 000 000
0   300 km
0   200 miles

▶ Pottery bowl from Tlapacoya in the valley of Mexico, 1200–900 B.C.E. The engraved design shows the head of a supernatural being with a snarling mouth. Coiling was the usual way to make pottery in Mesoamerica. Sometimes a previously made pot was used as the mold for a new one.

The earliest cultivated plants would have looked no different from wild ones. Then, as people began to select seed from the best plants to sow the following year, bigger and more productive varieties developed. Not all plants grown during this period were for food. One of the first to be cultivated was the bottle gourd. It was not good to eat, but when hollowed out and dried it made an excellent storage container.

The valley of Oaxaca
One of the areas where people began to change from gathering food to farming was the valley of Oaxaca in the Mexican state of the same name. This is a semidesert area, and for thousands of years nomadic hunters and gatherers camped in its caves and rock shelters. The remains of the food they ate are well preserved in the very dry conditions.

Squash and bottle gourds were the first crops, grown by 8000 B.C.E. By about 4300 B.C.E. corn was also being grown, but it was a long time before it grew in sufficient quantity and was nutritionally powerful enough (when combined with beans) to become a staple part of the diet. Similar changes were probably taking place all over Mesoamerica.

Gradually, people came to rely more and more on the food they grew themselves. They no longer needed to travel so far and were able to settle down in one place for much longer. One sign of this is the increasing presence of grinding stones to prepare corn. Another is the invention of pottery, which first appears of Mexico's Pacific coast about 2500 B.C.E. and quickly spread. By helping make their cooking easier, it may have encouraged people to start growing beans alongside other crops. Protein from plants such as beans was especially important in Mesoamerica because of the almost complete absence of domesticated animals.

The Formative period
The first permanent agriculturally based settlements in Mesoamerica date to about 1600 B.C.E. They consisted of small groups of thatched houses with clay and timber walls. San José Mogoté in the valley of Oaxaca was one of these settlements. It may have had some 200 inhabitants who planted gardens between their houses. This was the start of the period known as the Formative, when settled village life became the rule across Mesoamerica. Trade becomes more strongly evident at this time, but there is still little sign of some people being significantly less equal than others.

▲ Scrub landscape in the Tehuacán valley. This was an early corn-growing area.

▼ Five thousand years of farming changed the wild corn or maize cob (left) to the modern cob (right). The earliest cobs from the Tehuacán valley were only 1 in (2.5. cm) long.

Olmec Civilization

T HE OLMEC HEARTLAND LAY IN THE
tropical forests and swamps of the modern
Mexican states of Veracruz and Tabasco. The
origins of Olmec civilization remain mysterious, but
it probably arose from farming settlements that
flourished in the fertile river valleys.

From around 1200 B.C.E. the Olmec began to build
important ceremonial centers. These had earth
mounds and carved stone monuments. The main
centers are at San Lorenzo, La Venta, Laguna de los
Cerros, and Tres Zapotes.

Impressive stonework

The Olmec made colossal stone carvings—from
monuments to powerful human heads—and also
finely worked jade axes, figurines, and pendants.
They are all the more remarkable because the Olmec
had no metal tools. All carving must have been done
using chisels and grinding tools made of stone—a
very slow process.

Apart from the huge stone heads, thought to
portray individual rulers, most Olmec carvings are
of strange and terrifying supernatural beings. They
are often drawn from creatures of the tropical forest
and coast, which the Olmec knew and feared—the
jaguar, snake, caiman, harpy eagle, and shark. Most
important—and perhaps most terrifying —was a
half-human, half-animal "were-jaguar," often shown
as a howling baby with the sharp fangs and angry
eyes of a snarling jaguar.

Trade beyond the heartland

The Olmec had to look far across and even beyond
their heartland to obtain many of their raw
materials. Massive basalt boulders from the Tuxtla

▲ Olmec sculpture ranged from objects small enough to be
held in the hand, like this tiny lifelike jade bust, to the huge
stone heads over 7ft high at San Lorenzo and La Venta.

Mountains were brought to La Venta, perhaps floated
downriver by raft.

The same trade routes also carried Olmec
civilization to other areas. Olmec objects—or objects
in the Olmec style—have been found all the way
from central Mexico to Costa Rica. Although, for
reasons still unknown, the power of the Olmecs
faded from about 400 B.C.E., they influenced the
later great civilizations.

◀ Many Olmec carvings
depict strange or fearsome
supernatural beings. This jade
carving from Guatemala is of
the Shark God.

▶ The Olmec heartland's
warm wet climate produced
rich farming land, where corn
and other crops grew all year
around. But many of the raw
materials needed by the
Olmecs had to be acquired
through trade with areas
outside the heartland.

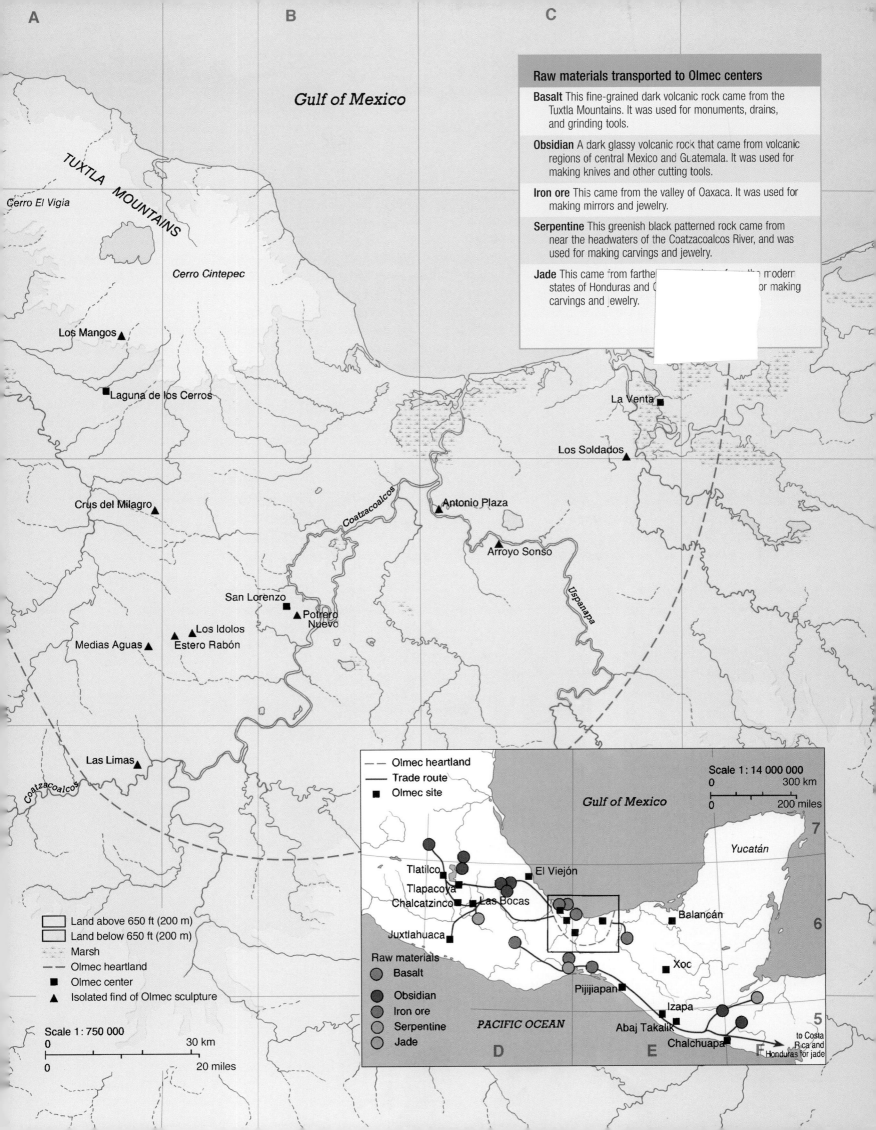

Gulf of Mexico

Raw materials transported to Olmec centers

Basalt This fine-grained dark volcanic rock came from the Tuxtla Mountains. It was used for monuments, drains, and grinding tools.

Obsidian A dark glassy volcanic rock that came from volcanic regions of central Mexico and Guatemala. It was used for making knives and other cutting tools.

Iron ore This came from the valley of Oaxaca. It was used for making mirrors and jewelry.

Serpentine This greenish black patterned rock came from near the headwaters of the Coatzacoalcos River, and was used for making carvings and jewelry.

Jade This came from farther _____ of _____ the modern states of Honduras and _____ for making carvings and jewelry.

TUXTLA MOUNTAINS

Cerro El Vigia

Cerro Cintepec

Los Mangos ▲

Laguna de los Cerros ■

Crus del Milagro ▲

Coatzacoalcos

Antonio Plaza ▲

La Venta ■

Los Soldados ▲

Arroyo Sonso ▲

Uspanapa

San Lorenzo

Potrero Nuevo ■

Los Idolos ▲

Medias Aguas ▲

Estero Rabón ▲

Las Limas ▲

Coatzacoalcos

Land above 650 ft (200 m)
Land below 650 ft (200 m)
Marsh
Olmec heartland
■ Olmec center
▲ Isolated find of Olmec sculpture

Scale 1 : 750 000
0 ———— 30 km
0 ———— 20 miles

Inset map legend:

--- Olmec heartland
— Trade route
■ Olmec site

Scale 1 : 14 000 000
0 ———— 300 km
0 ———— 200 miles

Gulf of Mexico

Yucatán

Tlatilco
Tlapacoya
Chalcatzinco
El Viejón
Las Bocas
Balancán
Juxtlahuaca
Xoc
Pijijiapan
PACIFIC OCEAN
Izapa
Abaj Takalik
Chalchuapa
to Costa Rica and Honduras for jade

Raw materials
◉ Basalt
◉ Obsidian
◉ Iron ore
◉ Serpentine
◉ Jade

Mesoamerican Sites 1

San Lorenzo

THE OLMEC CEREMONIAL CENTER OF SAN Lorenzo was built on a 165-foot- (50-m-) high, partly natural, partly human-made plateau. On the summit are nearly 200 earthen mounds grouped around rectangular courtyards. They were probably the bases on which houses were built. Larger mounds nearby may have been the bases for temples. The actual buildings, made of wood and thatch, have disappeared. A series of artificial pools was probably used for ceremonial bathing. An overflow system consisted of U-shaped sections of basalt drains laid end to end and fitted with lids.

The people of San Lorenzo

San Lorenzo probably flourished between 1200 and 900 B.C.E. The stone heads for which it is famous were probably those of rulers. At its peak San Lorenzo would have contained about 1,000 of the most important members of the community—rulers, nobles, and priests. Another 2,000 or so people may have lived in the surrounding area, in farming hamlets on the plain below the plateau. Around 900 B.C.E. San Lorenzo was violently destroyed. The stone sculptures were deliberately smashed and their remains buried. People continued to live there for a time but no more monuments were put up.

▲ This colossal stone head from San Lorenzo is one of a number found there and at La Venta. It may be a portrait of an Olmec ruler. It is carved from a basalt boulder brought 50 miles (80 km) from the Tuxtla Mountains.

La Venta

LA VENTA ROSE TO POWER WHEN SAN Lorenzo declined. It consists of a group of earthen mounds and enclosures built on an island in the swamps of northern Tabasco. After San Lorenzo was destroyed, La Venta was the Olmec's main political and religious center.

The largest mound at La Venta is the Great Pyramid, more than 100 feet (30 m) high and 420 feet (130 m) across its base. To its north lie a series of lower mounds and courtyards. Burials with rich grave goods have been found under some mounds, although the Great Pyramid has not yet been excavated. Because of the acidic soil, no skeletal remains survive.

Ceremonial buried offerings

The ceremonies performed here included the burial of offerings. Among the objects found are mirrors of highly polished iron ore and axheads, necklaces, and figurines carved from jade, serpentine, and granite. There are three mosaic pavements each made of 485 serpentine blocks, representing the face of a jaguar.

Around 400 B.C.E. La Venta was destroyed. Its monuments were brutally defaced, just as at San Lorenzo 500 years earlier. What led to this terrible destruction remains a mystery.

▶ These jade and serpentine figurines were found beneath a floor at La Venta. They had been arranged as if to show some kind of ceremony. They may be priests marching in procession or captives being brought before a ruler. About 100 years after they were buried, someone cut a hole in the floor above to inspect them. Their hiding place must have been carefully recorded, because the hole is directly over them.

▼ There are several of these large flat-topped basalt blocks at La Venta. Although often described as altars, they may have been used as thrones. The figure here, seated cross-legged in the niche, holds a rope that leads around the corner of the block to a bound prisoner.

Mesoamerican Sites 2

Teotihuacán—"Place of the Gods"

ABOUT 30 MILES (48 KM) NORTHEAST OF Mexico City lie the ruins of Teotihuacán. From about 150 C.E. it was the greatest of all the ancient American cities. More than 8 square miles (20 sq. km) of temples, palaces, and houses were laid out on a rectangular grid pattern. Some 125,000 people may have lived there. For hundreds of years the city dominated the valley of Mexico, and its influence reached across much of Mesoamerica.

Crossing the center of Teotihuacán is a great north–south roadway, now called the Avenue of the Dead. Ruins of more than 75 temples line its route, including the largest and oldest, the Pyramid of the Sun. It was built over a secret cave. Gods worshiped by later civilizations, such as Tlaloc the Rain God and Quetzalcoatl the Feathered Serpent, are shown in temple carvings and paintings. Archaeologists are only just beginning to realize that Teotihuacán's inhabitants used writing, like other Mesoamerican civilizations, but this is still not well understood.

A great center of craft and trade

Hundreds of workshops were scattered throughout the city. Skilled craftsmen made tools and weapons of obsidian or carved ornaments from shell and jade. Others made pottery, from heavy cooking pots to fine vases and incense burners. These goods found their way to other areas beyond Mesoamerica.

In return, merchants brought back turquoise from southwestern North America, shells and copal incense from the Gulf coast, and quetzal feathers from the lands of the Maya. Merchants from Teotihuacán may have settled in Maya cities, setting up trading posts and perhaps marrying into local families.

Much of Teotihuacán was destroyed by fire, and the city was largely abandoned around 500–550 C.E. Internal conflicts rather than external attack were probably responsible. But the city's greatness was not forgotten. Almost 1,000 years later Aztec emperors made pilgrimages to its temples.

◀ The Pyramid of the Sun as it is now. Rising to a height of more than 200 ft (60 m), it towers over the city and can be seen from afar.

▶ The Pyramid of the Sun in its heyday. To the left, at the northern end of the Avenue of the Dead, is the smaller Pyramid of the Moon, where evidence of sacrificial victims has been found. Beyond the Pyramid of the Sun lay the marketplace and the Temple of Quetzalcoatl (not shown).

Teotihuacán

Maya Civilization

THE MAYA CIVILIZATION WAS UNDOUBTEDLY the greatest of the ancient Americas. It was probably from the Olmecs that the Maya learned the systems of writing and recording time that they later perfected.

As well as their scientific achievements, the Maya are famous for great stone-built cities with towering temple-pyramids and palaces. Many of these cities have been reclaimed from the jungle and restored to some of their former glory.

City-states and warrior kings

Maya cities were independent states, each with its own ruling dynasty. Rulers, who were usually male, passed succession from father to eldest son. They claimed descent from the gods and inscribed their ancestry on monuments or walls.

The city-states were often at war—not just to gain territory, but also to take prisoners. Important ceremonies, such as a ruler's accession to the throne, included the offering of a human sacrifice to the gods, for which a plentiful supply of prisoners was needed.

Time and astrology

Because ancestry was important, the Maya needed a system for recording time. Their system is known as the Long Count. A date was calculated by counting up the number of days that had elapsed since a fixed starting point. For reasons that we do not know, this starting point corresponds to the year 3114 B.C.E. in our calendar.

The Maya had two calendars. One was of 365 days, divided into 18 months of 20 days each, with an extra five days at the end. The other was a sacred calendar consisting of 260 days, divided into 13 weeks of 20 days. It was used to foretell the future and avoid bad luck.

Only priests trained in astrology could read the sacred calendar, and people consulted them before important events. So, if a child was born on an unlucky day, his naming ceremony could be put off until a luckier one, to ensure his good fortune.

▲ Abandoned for centuries, the great temple-pyramids of Tikal rise above the jungle. The largest Maya city, Tikal is famous for its splendid stone architecture. In the eighth and ninth centuries C.E., 90,000 people may have lived here.

Numbers and calendars

The Maya used three basic symbols for numbers: a stylized shell for zero, a dot for one, and a bar for five (4 dots = 4; 2 bars and a dot = 11; and so on). Time was recorded in units of 144,000 days (*baktun*), 7,200 days (*katun*), 360 days (*tun*), 20 days (*uinal*), and 1 day (*kin*). Each of these calendar units was represented by a different glyph (picture symbol). An example of a glyph is shown on page 65.

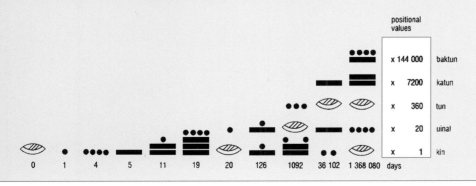

positional values		
x 144 000	baktun
x 7200	katun
x 360	tun
x 20	uinal
x 1	kin

0   1   4   5   11   19   20   126   1092   36 102   1 368 080   days

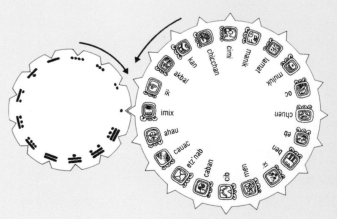

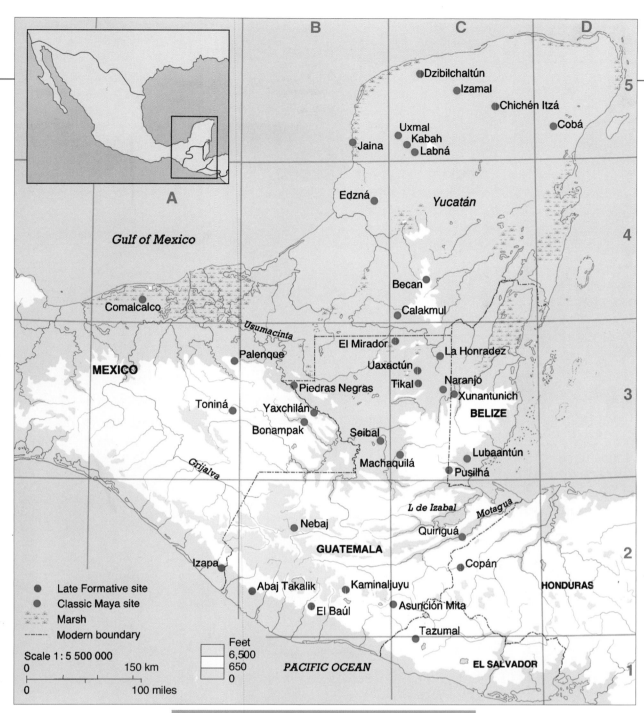

B **C** **D**

5

4

3

2

1

Dzibilchaltún
Izamal
Chichén Itzá
Uxmal
Kabah
Jaina
Labná
Cobá

Edzná

Yucatán

Gulf of Mexico

Becan
Calakmul

Comalcalco

Usumacinta

El Mirador
La Honradez
Palenque
Uaxactún
Naranjo
Piedras Negras
Tikal
Xunantunich
Toniná
Yaxchilán
BELIZE
Bonampak
Seibal
Machaquilá
Lubaantún
Pusilhá

Grijalva

L de Izabal
Motagua

Nebaj
Quiriguá
GUATEMALA

Izapa
Copán
HONDURAS

● Late Formative site
● Classic Maya site
░ Marsh
‒ ‒ Modern boundary

Abaj Takalik
Kaminaljuyu
El Baúl
Asunción Mita

Scale 1 : 5 500 000
0   150 km
0   100 miles

Feet
6,500
650
0

Tazumal
EL SALVADOR

PACIFIC OCEAN

MEXICO

◄ For more than 500 years Maya civilization flourished in three regions: in the highlands of Guatemala, in the low-lying tropical rain forests of northern Guatemala and Belize, and in the Yucatán peninsula. Most cities were independent states although their rulers were often linked by marriage.

▼ The Maya did not have an alphabet. They wrote in pictures, or glyphs. Most Maya inscriptions concern important events in the lives of Maya rulers. The scene shown here is carved on a stone lintel at Yaxchilán. The top and middle glyphs tell how on a certain day Bird Jaguar, the ruler of Yaxchilán, took two important prisoners. The prisoners' names are written on their thighs

Calendar

This diagram shows how the sacred 260-day calendar worked. The wheel on the left has 13 numbers. The wheel on the right has 20 named days. The wheels turn so that each number fits in with a day. The week starts on 1 *imix*. The next day is 2 *ik*, and so on. After 13 days the left-hand wheel comes around to 1 again to begin a new week. This time the week starts on 1 *ix*.

The Maya c.300 B.C.E.–1541 C.E.

300 B.C.E.–300 C.E. Early Maya people influenced by outposts of Olmec civilization at Izapa, Abaj Takalik, El Baúl, and Kaminaljuyu. Ceremonial centers built at sites in the southern lowlands such as Tikal, Uaxactún, and El Mirador.

300–800 The golden age of Maya civilization. Architecture, art, and science flourish at great cities like Copán, Quiriguá, Naranjo, Piedras Negras, Uxmal, Cobá, and Chichén Itzá.

800–900 Mayan civilization in the southern lowlands collapsed, for reasons unknown. Many cities were abandoned.

c.980 Toltecs invade Yucatán and make Chichén Itzá their capital. The Maya civilization survives under Toltec rule.

1200–1500 New Maya capital at Mayapan. Decline of Maya civilization.

1517–1541 Spanish conquest of Guatemala and Yucatán.

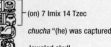
(on) 7 Imix 14 Tzec
chucha "(he) was captured"
Jeweled skull

"captor of"
second captive

u bac "the captive of"
Bird Jaguar
Lord of Yaxchilán

Palenque

PALENQUE WAS THE MOST WESTERLY OF the Maya city-states. It lies in the modern Mexican state of Chiapas among the wooded foothills overlooking the coastal plain that stretches to the Gulf of Mexico.

Until about 600 C.E. Palenque was small and unimportant. In 615 a new ruler came to the throne. His name was Pacal and he was only 12 years old at the time of his accession. During his long reign and those of his two sons (named Chan-Bahlum and

▼ The ceremonial center at Palenque with the Temple of the Sun in the foreground. The Temple of the Inscriptions is in the center. (Stone panels have hieroglyphs telling the story of the life of Pacal, whose tomb lies at the base of the pyramid.) The palace is on the right.

◄ The palace at Palenque was built over a period of about 100 years. The tower was probably used as an observatory by astronomers. It may also have been a watchtower because, from the top story, it is possible to survey the whole plain to the north.

Kan-Xul II), the city became large and powerful, and a center of government for the surrounding area.

Pacal's tomb

Palenque contains many fine buildings that are richly decorated with painted plasterwork, or stucco. One of the most splendid is the Temple of the Inscriptions. It is set on top of a nine-tiered pyramid that was built by Pacal to house his own tomb. According to Maya mythology, the underworld had nine levels and the nine tiers of the pyramid probably represent this.

Stone panels in the temple are carved with glyphs in human or animal form, and long hieroglyphic inscriptions relating to Pacal's life and ancestry. Astronomers calculated the dates of mythical events going back many thousands of years.

Pacal died in 683 at the age of 80. He was buried in a stone sarcophagus underneath the base of the pyramid. The scene carved on the sarcophagus lid shows him entering the underworld. The painted

stucco panels that decorate the tomb walls depict the nine Lords of the Night who ruled the underworld.

The Palenque palace

The city continued to grow during the reigns of Pacal's sons. Several new temples were built. The palace was enlarged and the graceful four-story tower, which was unique in Maya architecture, was added. The palace even had its own water supply, brought from the nearby Otulum River along a stone-lined aqueduct.

The palace may have been a ceremonial center rather than a royal residence. Stone carvings and decorative moldings on the walls show some of these ceremonies. Some celebrate the accessions of rulers and give us an idea of the luxury of court life. Others, such as the depiction of a row of captives along a staircase wall, are a reminder that warfare was a significant part of Maya life and probably instrumental in bringing about the collapse of lowland civilization in the ninth century.

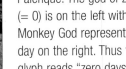

▲ This mosaic jade mask may portray Pacal himself. It was found lying on top of his sarcophagus.

► This glyph is part of a date inscribed on a wall at Palenque. The god of zero (= 0) is on the left with the Monkey God representing day on the right. Thus the glyph reads "zero days."

The Toltecs

"The Toltecs were wise. Their works were all good, all perfect, all wonderful, all marvelous; their houses beautiful, tiled in mosaics, stuccoed, smoothed, very marvelous . . . they were thinkers, for they originated the year count, the day count; they established the way in which the night, the day, would work."

HERE IS THE AZTEC VIEW OF THE TOLTECS, written down after the Conquest by a Spanish priest, Bernardino de Sahagún. Perhaps not surprisingly, the Aztecs, including their emperor, claimed descent from Toltec ancestors!

The origins of the Toltecs

Although the Aztecs looked back to the time of the Toltecs as a golden age of peace and prosperity, this does not always fit in with what archaeologists have found. Far from being peace-loving, the Toltecs seem to have been fierce and warlike. They ruled by force over much of central Mexico in the 11th and 12th centuries and often fought among themselves.

The origins of the Toltecs are mysterious. They seem to have been a mixture of different groups. From the rocky desert of northern Mexico came the Tolteca-Chichimeca, barbarian nomads who lived by hunting and gathering and perhaps a little farming. The other group, the Tolteca-Nonoalca, came from farther south. Some writers think that they may have been sculptors and craftsmen, brought in to help build the city of Tula.

Tula—The Toltec capital

Tula was built in a commanding position on a high ridge about 40 miles (65 km) northwest of modern Mexico City. Its most impressive building is undoubtedly the four-tiered temple-pyramid (archaeologists have named it Pyramid B).

Visitors to the temple in its heyday first passed through a colonnaded hall, decorated with relief carvings of marching warriors. They entered the temple itself through a doorway flanked by stone pillars in the form of Feathered Serpents (see page 60). The temple roof was supported on the heads of four colossal stone warriors.

At the temple and in other parts of the city there were strange stone figures called Chac Mools. They take the form of warriors lying on their backs. Bowls carved on their chests were probably meant for sacrificial offerings.

Many things in Tula point to the Toltecs' warlike nature. Besides the painted reliefs and statues of

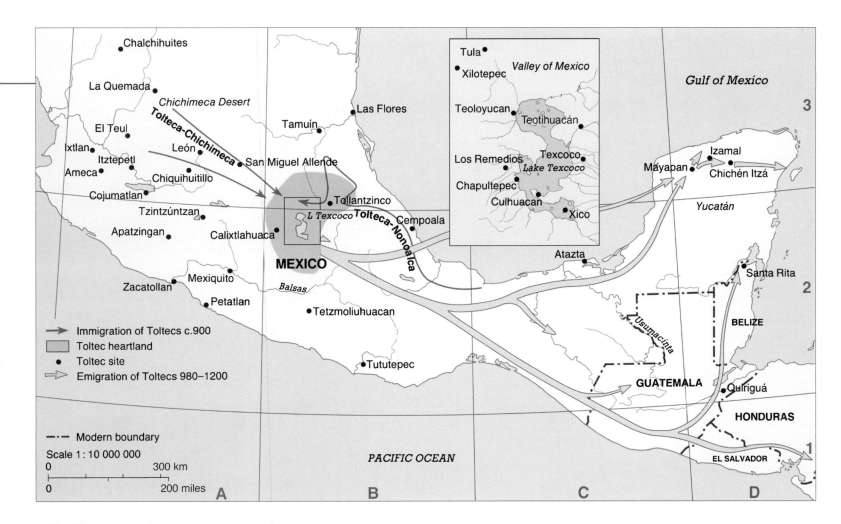

Map labels:

Chalchihuites
La Quemada
Chichimeca Desert
Tolteca-Chichimeca
El Teul
Ixtlan
Itztepetl
León
Ameca
Chiquihuitillo
San Miguel Allende
Cojumatlan
Tzintzúntzan
Apatzingan
Calixtlahuaca
MEXICO
L. Texcoco
Tolteca-Nonoalca
Tollantzinco
Cempoala
Balsas
Zacatollan
Mexiquito
Petatlan
Tetzmoliuhuacan
Tututepec

Tamuín
Las Flores

Gulf of Mexico

Tula
Xilotepec
Valley of Mexico
Teoloyucan
Teotihuacán
Los Remedios
Texcoco
Lake Texcoco
Chapultepec
Culhuacan
Xico

Atazta
Usumacinta
Mayapan
Izamal
Chichén Itzá
Yucatán
Santa Rita
BELIZE
GUATEMALA
Quiriguá
HONDURAS
EL SALVADOR

PACIFIC OCEAN

→ Immigration of Toltecs c.900
▨ Toltec heartland
• Toltec site
⇨ Emigration of Toltecs 980–1200

–·–· Modern boundary
Scale 1 : 10 000 000
0 — 300 km
0 — 200 miles

A   B   C   D

3
2
1

▲ The Toltecs were a mixture of nomadic tribes from the Chichimeca Desert and Nonoalca people from the modern state of Oaxaca and the Gulf Coast. During the 10th and 11th centuries they spread into many parts of Mesoamerica.

◀ One of four stone figures that supported the roof of the temple of Pyramid B, Tula. More than 13 ft (4 m) high, it consists of four sections of basalt pegged together. It represents a Toltec warrior armed with shield, spear, and *atlatl* (spear thrower).

▶ This almost life-size clay figure represents Xipe Totec, the god of vegetation and planting. At springtime ceremonies he was impersonated by a priest wearing the flayed skin of a human sacrificial victim.

Rise and decline of the Toltecs

c.900 Chichimeca nomads enter valley of Mexico.

c.950 They join with the Nonoalca people from the south to found the city of Tula.

c.1000 The Maya city of Chichén Itzá was taken over by foreigners, perhaps Toltecs from Tula (according to Maya texts).

1168 Tula destroyed by Chichimeca invaders.

c.1200 Power of Chichén Itzá declines. The Maya build a new capital at Mayapan.

warriors, there are carvings of skulls and crossbones, serpents swallowing skeletons, eagles devouring hearts, and prowling jaguars and coyotes. (These last three were symbols of the elite corps in Aztec times.)

The destruction of Tula

In 1168 Tula was attacked by fierce nomads who, like the Toltecs themselves, came from the northern desert. The temples and palaces were looted and the great stone warriors hurled to the ground. The inhabitants fled, leaving Tula deserted and in ruins. Little remains of the immense ceremonial platform with its serpent columns. Tula's golden age lasted only about 200 years, but its warlike sun-worshiping ethos survived through adoption by the Aztecs.

Chichén Itzá

CHICHÉN ITZÁ WAS ONE OF THE GREATEST Maya centers of the Yucatán peninsula, but by 1200 C.E. it went into decline. Throughout its history different peoples left their mark. According to Aztec legend, the Toltec city of Tula was first ruled by a wise and peace-loving king named Topiltzin Quetzalcoatl. But the warlike god Tezcatlipoca challenged his authority and he was forced to flee from the city. With his followers, the king set sail across the Gulf of Mexico on a raft made of serpents, promising that he would come back one day to reclaim his kingdom.

The Toltecs in Yucatán

The first Bishop of Yucatán, Diego de Landa, wrote in the mid-16th century:

> "It is believed among the Indians that with the Itzas who occupied Chichén Itzá, there reigned a great lord named Kukulcan . . . They say that he arrived from the west . . . he was regarded in Mexico as one of their gods and called Quetzalcoatl; and they also considered him a god in Yucatán on account of his being a just statesman."

The most impressive building in Chichén Itzá is the Castillo (castle) that stands in the center of the main plaza. It is, in fact, a temple-pyramid, dedicated to Quetzalcoatl. Excavations in the 1930s found that the Castillo had been built over an earlier temple-pyramid. Some people have suggested that this first pyramid may house a royal burial.

The "Well of Sacrifice"

From the main plaza a causeway leads to the Sacred Cenote, a natural well dedicated to the rain god. Pilgrimages to the well continued long after the Spanish Conquest. Offerings dredged from its depths around 1900 spanned a period of more than 1,000 years. These offerings included copal incense, carved jade, and gold disks embossed with battle scenes. Bones, too, were recovered, showing that offerings to the rain god included human sacrifice.

The Great Ballcourt

A ballgame, *tlachti*, was played all over Mesoamerica. Two opposing teams played with a large solid rubber ball in a specially made court. At Paso de la Amada

▼ View across the main plaza at Chichén Itzá, with a jaguar throne standing in the foreground. In the background rises the Pyramid of Kukulcan or Quetzalcoatl, usually called the Castillo. It is built in nine tiers with a staircase on each side.

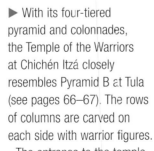
◀ A small carved jade plaque, one of many objects dredged up from the Well of Sacrifice at Chichén Itzá.

▼ This stone sculpture shows a human face framed by the gaping jaws of an animal. It may represent a high-ranking warrior wearing a wooden helmet carved in the form of a jaguar. Aztec and Toltec warriors wore helmets of this type.

in Chiapas, Mexico, archaeologists have found possibly the oldest ballcourt in the Americas, dating from about 1700 B.C.E.—far older than any previously excavated ballcourt. The 260-foot- (80-m-) court was flanked by benches for spectators.

The Great Ballcourt at Chichén Itzá is the largest of all known ballcourts. The playing area is 480 feet (146 m) long and 120 feet (37 m) wide, about the area of a modern soccer field.

The game seems to have been a kind of basketball. The object was to knock the ball through a stone ring set high on the court wall. At Chichén Itzá this must have been especially difficult, since there the rings are about 26 feet (8 m) above the floor of the court.

Players were not allowed to touch the ball with their hands, only with their hips and knees. They wore protective clothing, including a heavy belt made of wood and leather, and leather hip pads, knee pads, and gloves. Even so, the game was so rough that players were often injured or even killed.

Spectators flocked to the ballcourt to cheer on their favorite team and place bets. These could be enormous: "gold, turquoise, slaves, rich mantles, even cornfields and houses . . ." wrote de Sahagún (see page 66). But the game was not simply a test of strength and skill. For the players it could be, quite literally, a contest to the death. Carvings around the walls of the Great Ballcourt at Chichén Itzá show members of the winning team sacrificing a defeated opponent by cutting off his head.

▶ With its four-tiered pyramid and colonnades, the Temple of the Warriors at Chichén Itzá closely resembles Pyramid B at Tula (see pages 66–67). The rows of columns are carved on each side with warrior figures.

The entrance to the temple, at the top of the steps, is guarded by a reclining Chac Mool figure, flanked by two Feathered Serpents, the symbol for Quetzalcoatl.

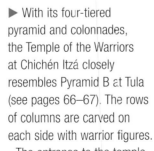

The Aztec Empire

THE AZTECS CLAIMED TO BE DESCENDED from nomadic barbarians from northern Mexico. Their wanderings were guided by their tribal god Huitzilopochtli whose image they carried with them.

About 1300 C.E. they came to Lake Texcoco in the valley of Mexico. Already there were powerful city-states here. For a time the Aztecs worked as serfs for some of the rulers.

The Aztec empire 1345–1521

1345 Aztecs found Tenochtitlán on Lake Texcoco.

1428 Triple Alliance formed (Texcoco, Tenochtitlán, and Tlacopán). Aztecs control valley of Mexico.

1440–68 Emperor Montezuma I expands empire to the Gulf of Mexico.

1486–1502 Emperor Ahuizotl expands empire to the Pacific coast and the borders of Guatemala.

1519 Spanish invaders land in Mexico.

1520–21 Emperor Montezuma II killed. Aztec empire destroyed.

▼ By 1502 the Aztec empire was at its full extent. Teotitlán, Tlaxcallan, and the Tarascan kingdom stayed independent states. Conquered provinces had to pay an annual tribute to the empire, such as food or luxury goods—jaguar skins and quetzal feathers.

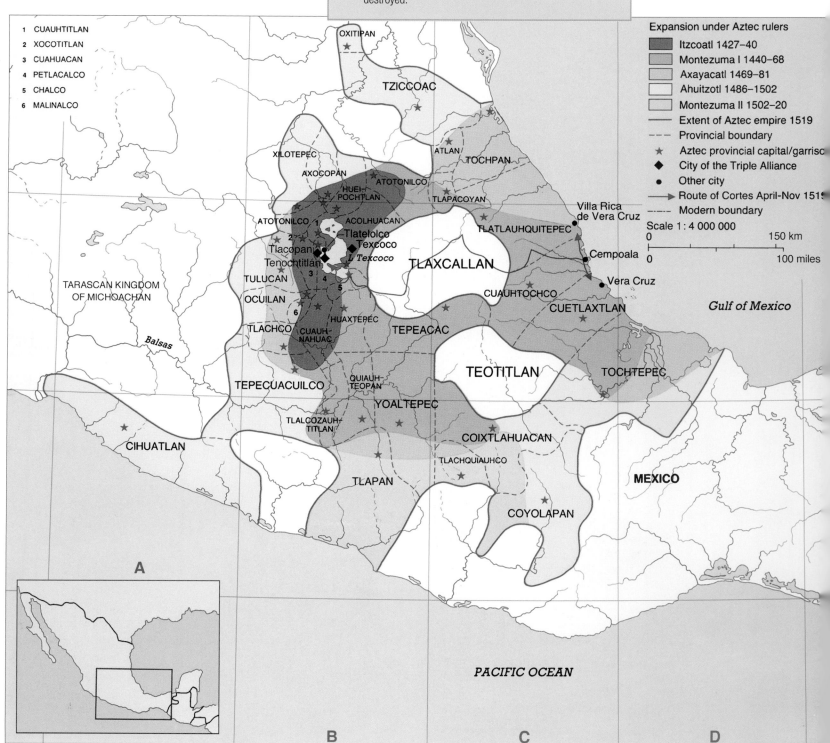

1 CUAUHTITLAN
2 XOCOTITLAN
3 CUAHUACAN
4 PETLACALCO
5 CHALCO
6 MALINALCO

Expansion under Aztec rulers
- Itzcoatl 1427–40
- Montezuma I 1440–68
- Axayacatl 1469–81
- Ahuitzotl 1486–1502
- Montezuma II 1502–20
- Extent of Aztec empire 1519
- Provincial boundary
- ★ Aztec provincial capital/garriso
- ◆ City of the Triple Alliance
- • Other city
- Route of Cortes April–Nov 151
- Modern boundary

Scale 1 : 4 000 000

0   150 km
0   100 miles

In 1345 the Aztecs settled on some swampy islands near the western shore of Lake Texcoco. A tribal prophecy had foretold that they would one day build a great city where an eagle, holding a snake, perched on a prickly pear cactus. The Aztecs believed these islands to be the place. On land reclaimed from the swamp they built houses of cane and thatch with a temple for their god. They called the settlement Tenochtitlán ("place of the prickly pear cactus").

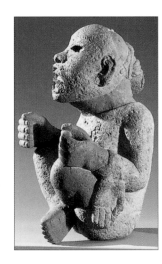

▶ A priest impersonating Xipe Totec, god of planting (a Toltec goc whom the Aztecs adopted). He wore the flayed skin of a sacrificial victim for 20 days. The shedding of the skin symbolized the sprouting in spring of a new shoot from the husk of an old seed.

▼ The skull of a captive chosen to impersonate the supreme god Tezcatlipoca ("Smoking Mirror") for one year. When the year was up, he was killed as a sacrifice to the god.

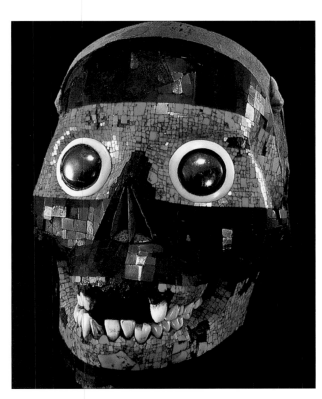

The Aztecs came to power by serving as mercenaries for the neighboring city-state of Atzcapotzalco. They eventually became so strong and so experienced in war that in 1428 they were able to defeat Atzcapotzalco and take control of all of its territories.

By forming the Triple Alliance (see map) they extended their power over the whole valley of Mexico. By 1500 the Aztecs controlled an empire of some 10 million people that stretched from coast to coast and from the valley of Mexico in the northwest to Guatemala in the southeast.

The Aztec army

The Aztecs won their vast empire by war, with a large, well-organized and well-equipped army. Like a modern army, it was divided into units under the command of officers, or war chiefs.

Officers were appointed entirely on merit. Some were elected by those they commanded. Others won their rank by taking captives in battle. The Aztecs needed captives, even in peaceful times, to use as sacrifices to the gods. The so-called "Flowery Wars" were arranged with other states with the aim of obtaining such captives.

All boys over the age of 15, except those intending to be priests, trained as warriors. The army's main weapon was the spear and spear thrower, or *atlatl*, but slings and bows and arrows were also used. Most fearsome of all was the *macahuitl*, a flat wooden club edged with razor-sharp blades of obsidian.

Every warrior wore a tunic of quilted cotton and carried a shield of the same material over a cane frame. High-ranking warriors, such as the Jaguar Knights or Eagle knights, wore carved wooden helmets and animal skin or feather costumes.

The emperor

The Aztec emperor was elected from among members of the royal family by a council of nobles, priests, and warriors. His actual title was Tlatoani, meaning "Speaker."

Because of the records kept by the Spanish invaders, the emperor about whom we know most is the last one, Montezuma II. People treated him as a god. No one was allowed to look directly at his face. Even great nobles had to enter his presence barefoot and with bowed heads. He traveled in a litter carried on the shoulders of his nobles. If he walked, they swept and then covered the ground with cloths so that the feet of the godlike ruler need not touch it.

The Aztec Capital

"When we saw so many cities and villages built both on the water and on dry land . . . we could not resist our admiration . . . because of the high towers, cues [pyramids] and other buildings, all of masonry, which rose from the water. Some of our soldiers asked if [it] was not a dream."

WITH THESE WORDS BERNAL DIAZ, A soldier with Hernán Cortés (see page 12), recalled his first enchanted glimpse of Tenochtitlán in 1519. Built on swampy islands in Lake Texcoco, it had become a wealthy and powerful city of more than half a million people. There were towering temples and palaces, bustling markets, and suburbs of houses and gardens. Produce to feed the city was grown on *chinampas*, or "floating gardens."

▼ Aztec nobles and warriors survey the ceremonial center of Tenochtitlán. The temple of Quetzalcoatl is before them, and beyond it is the great double temple-pyramid dedicated to Huitzilopochtli, the God of War, and Tlaloc, the Rain God. Nearby is the *tzompantli*, or skull rack, where the heads of sacrificial victims were put on display. In the distance are groups of houses and gardens.

The great market at Tenochtitlán

Canoes thronged the lake and the city's network of canals, bringing goods and produce from all over the empire to the great market. Each day more than 60,000 people came to trade. Stallholders offered food and clothing of all kinds, pottery cups and dishes, tobacco pipes, and cigarettes. There were luxury goods—gold, silver, jade, and feathers. Slaves were displayed for sale like captive animals in wooden cages.

Most people bartered what they had for what they wanted. The Aztecs had no money, but there were some fixed units of value, ranging from cocoa beans (small change) to high-value woven mantles (cloaks) or jade necklaces (one mantle was equal to 100 cocoa beans).

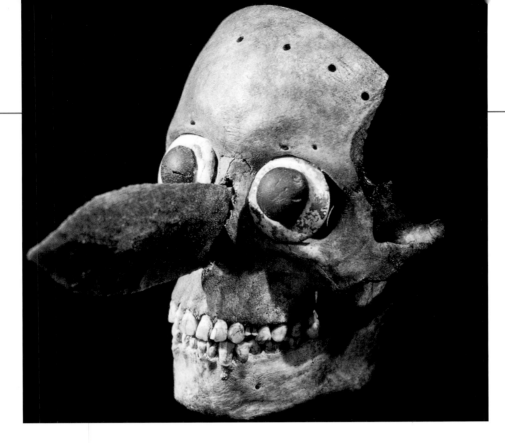

◄ This Aztec skull-mask is made more sinister-looking by the sacrificial knife fixed into the nose socket. Razor-sharp stone knives like this were used in ceremonies to kill human victims.

The Aztecs paid homage to the gods by making them many kinds of offerings. The most important offering was human blood. The Aztecs believed that, unless the gods were given this "food," the world would come to an end.

The Antilles and Colombia

THE "INDIANS" WHO CAME TO GREET THE explorer Christopher Columbus when he landed in the Bahamas during his first voyage to the New World in 1492 were the Arawak. Columbus noted in his log-book:

"I gave some of them red caps and glass beads which they hung round their necks, also many other trifles. These things pleased them greatly and they became marvelously friendly to us."

The Arawak people were fishermen and hunters, who traveled among the Caribbean islands in large canoes. They were also farmers and grew manioc, corn, beans, and peppers in the fields near their villages of round thatched houses. They also grew

▼ Lake Guatavita in the mountains of Colombia, near Bogotá. The Muisca Indians believed it to be the home of a powerful god. Muisca rulers, covered in gold dust, sailed out into the lake to throw in offerings of gold and jewels. This was the origin of the legend of El Dorado ("the Gilded One").

Many gold objects have been dredged from the lake, but it has never been successfully drained. The cut through the hill on the far side of the lake was part of a scheme to drain it in the 1580s. Gold and jewels were recovered, but this attempt was stopped when the cut collapsed, killing many workmen.

◄ ▲ Carved stone figures found near the mountain village of San Agustín, southern Colombia. More than 300 of these figures are scattered over a wide area. Some stand alone or in groups on hillsides. Others have been found in stone tombs. Many depict half-human, half-jaguar beings with bared fangs.

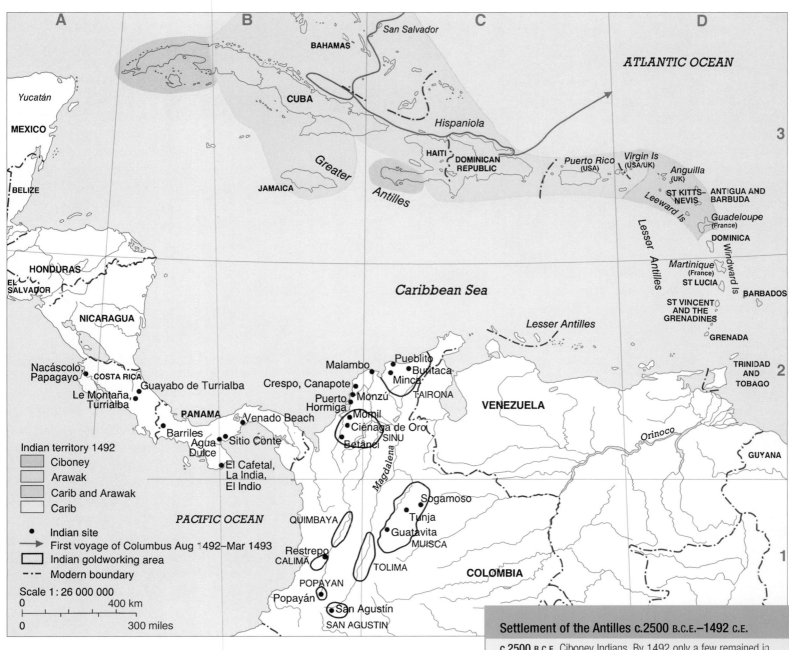

Indian territory 1492
- Ciboney
- Arawak
- Carib and Arawak
- Carib

- • Indian site
- → First voyage of Columbus Aug 1492–Mar 1493
- ▭ Indian goldworking area
- –·– Modern boundary

Scale 1 : 26 000 000

0 _____ 400 km

0 _____ 300 miles

▲ The Ciboney, Arawak, and Carib originally came to the Antilles by canoe or raft from northeastern Venezuela via Trinidad. Other peoples settled in the tropical lowlands and fertile river valleys of Colombia, living in large well-built towns. They were farmers and also skillful goldsmiths. In some areas gold was worked 1,000 years before the Spanish Conquest.

cotton, from which they made cloth and the hammocks in which they slept.

Other Native Americans were in the Antilles when Columbus arrived. The earliest inhabitants, the Ciboney, were by then few in number, having been largely driven out by the Arawak. More threatening to the Arawak were the Carib, a fierce warlike people who had the reputation of being cannibals.

The friendliness that had marked the first meeting between the Native Americans and Columbus was not to last, however. In less than 100 years the Arawak had vanished from the Caribbean islands, victims of European disease and warfare.

The Central Andes

THE EARLIEST INHABITANTS OF THE ANDES hunted animals and collected wild plant food, but fishing and farming gradually became more important. Fishing nets were made from cotton twine, and floats from hollowed-out gourds. Farmers grew crops such as squash, beans, chili peppers, corn (introduced from Mesoamerica), and potatoes. They kept dogs as pets and for hunting, and they raised ducks and guinea pigs for food. Herds of llamas and alpacas were bred for their wool and meat, and llamas were also used as pack animals.

Some of the greatest civilizations in the New World developed in this area, such as the Moche and Chimu along the coast and the Inca in the highlands. Early peoples often influenced those who came later. When the Inca conquered the Chimu around 1470, for example, they borrowed much of their art and way of life.

The Chavín civilization

People had already begun building large ceremonial complexes on Peru's desert coast by 3000 B.C.E., supported in part by very rich offshore fisheries. Much later the site of Chavín de Huantar, which flourished between 400 and 200 B.C.E., developed an art style, religious beliefs, and new technologies in textile and metal production that spread across large parts of Peru.

At the site's center lay a large temple, which was honeycombed with rooms and passages connected by stairways. It was probably a pilgrimage center for people from afar.

Tombs at Paracas

The Paracas peninsula is probably best known for the large number of tombs that have been found there, dating from between 700 and 200 B.C.E. The tombs contained mummified bodies wrapped in layers of cloth to form bundles.

The bundles included sets of cotton garments—for example, shirts, mantles, loin cloths, and turbans. Many of the garments were beautifully embroidered with strange mythical creatures, birds, and animals.

◀ This carved stone head is one of several fixed into the walls of the temple at Chavín de Huantar. It depicts a supernatural creature, partly human, but with the fangs of a jaguar. Other carvings here show eagles, snakes, caimans, or humans with the features of these animals. The Chavín art style spread over much of Peru.

▼ The Native Americans obtained most of their gold by panning in highland streams and rivers. They used "digging sticks" (straight, pointed sticks) to loosen and break up the earth and gravel, which they then washed in shallow wooden trays. In some areas they also dug shafts to mine veins of quartz to extract gold. Silver and copper ores were dug from pits and smelted in clay furnaces.

Copper and bronze were used to make weapons and tools, while gold and silver was mainly for jewelry and ceremonial objects.

◀ Ceremonial knife *tumi* from the Lambayeque valley, northern Peru, about 1200 C.E. The handle may show the Sun God. The headdress is inlaid with turquoise.

▶ Embroidery from a Paracas mummy bundle. It shows a supernatural being wearing a headband of sheet gold, a kind that has been found in burials.

▼ A pendant of cast tumbaga (a gold–copper alloy), made in the Tairona area of Colombia about 1000 C.E. It may represent a supernatural being (part human, part bat) or a priest wearing a bat mask.

The colors of the wool embroidery remain rich and vivid today, because the dry desert air helped preserve them.

Metalworking in the Andes

The Andean region was the greatest center of metalworking in America. According to early Spanish writers, the Inca thought of gold as "the sweat of the sun" and silver as "the tears of the moon."

The earliest metalwork found—a few scraps of gold foil—dates from about 1500 B.C.E. Later on, gold, silver, copper, and platinum were all worked, and mixed with one another to form alloys. Copper was also alloyed with tin to make bronze.

Smiths worked the metal by hammering it into thin sheets. Shapes were cut to make masks, crowns, ear ornaments, necklaces, and pins. Figurines were also cast in molds.

Nazca: Lines in the Desert

THE NAZCA PEOPLE ARE NAMED FOR sites in the Nazca valley on the south coast of Peru. They lived in several of the coastal river valleys from about 200 B.C.E. to 650 C.E.

The Nazca may have been related to the people who produced the textiles and other grave goods found at Paracas. The designs used by the Nazca on their textiles and pottery are very similar to those of Paracas. Quantities of both Paracas and Nazca pottery have been found at Ocucje in the Ica valley.

The ordinary people lived in small villages. Unlike those who lived in the mountains, the coastal people did not have supplies of good stone for building

▼ The Nazca people made some of the finest pottery in the New World. Painted in rich colors, the pots depict gods and people, animals, birds, and plants. This jar, made in the form of a supernatural being, is painted with strange monsters and "trophy heads," probably those of sacrificed captives.

purposes. The Nazca built their houses of wattle and daub or adobe bricks.

The most important Nazca site is the ceremonial center of Cuachi in the Nazca valley. The site consists of several terraced pyramids that are, in fact, natural hills faced with adobe bricks. The largest of these pyramids is 65 feet (20 m) high. Around it were once plazas, rooms, and tombs.

The Nazca lines

Among the most fascinating of all archaeological puzzles are the so-called Nazca lines that cover an area of almost 200 square miles (500 sq. km) northwest of the modern town of Nazca. They were created by removing the dark surface stones to expose the lighter ground below.

The lines vary from 600 yards (550 m) to more than 5 miles (8 km) in length. Some of them join to form geometric shapes such as squares or triangles. Others cross one another or come together at a central point.

Not all the lines are straight, however. Some are in the form of plants and animals—a tree, birds, a spider, a killer whale, and a monkey with a long spiraling tail. Since there is no rain to disturb the ground in this desert area, the lines remain just as they were made more than 1,000 years ago.

Gods and stars

Because of their large size, the shapes made by the lines are difficult to recognize on the ground. It was not until the 1920s, when they were viewed from an airplane, that their complete outlines were finally discovered. One of the many puzzles surrounding the lines is how they were plotted so accurately, for the people who made them could only ever have seen them from the ground.

Just as mysterious as how the lines were made is why they were made. Some writers have suggested that, since they are completely visible only from the air, they may have been offerings to the sky gods. Another theory is that the lines were ritual pathways, pointing to the sun at times when seasonal rains were likely.

The Nazca may have walked the paths, remarking them in seasonal ceremonies. Farmers may have used them as a calendar to predict the weather and so prepare for the irrigation of crops. (Rain in the mountains would bring floodwater to these dry areas.) Similar markings have been found elsewhere in Peru and in Chile, about 500 miles (800 km) away.

▶ Nazca outlines of a figure (right) and a cactus (far right). The "astronaut drawing" has inspired many theories about the lines' origin and purpose.

▼ Some Nazca lines align with the setting sun at times of the year such as the winter solstice. These lines may have been laid out by astronomers to help them calculate the movement of the planets.

Central Andean Sites

The Moche people

THE SITE OF MOCHE IS ON THE NORTHERN coast of Peru, near the modern city of Trujillo. It was the ceremonial and administrative capital of the Moche people who lived in this area between the second and eighth centuries C.E.

The Moche were farmers, growing a variety of crops in the river valleys. They built canals and aqueducts to irrigate their fields. Many of these are great feats of engineering, and some are still in use today. They built reed boats for use on inland waterways and also at sea, for trading activities with neighboring peoples.

We know a great deal about the Moche from pottery that has been found in their graves. Modeled and painted decoration depicts gods, people, houses, plants, and animals. Their everyday activities—such as hunting, fishing, or weaving—as well as rituals and ceremonies are shown.

Temples and pyramids

The Moche also built large temples. The most impressive of them are the great twin adobe pyramids at Moche itself. They are known as the Huaca del Sol (Temple of the Sun) and the Huaca de la Luna (Temple of the Moon). (These names were given by the Spanish and are misleading—both complexes were probably royal residences, complete with tombs and the quarters and workshops of craftsmen and retainers.) Both sites consist of terraced platforms and the larger—the Huaca del Sol—has a terraced pyramid on top of it.

The Huaca de la Luna lies at the foot of a hill, Cerro Blanco. It stands about 70 feet (21 m) high and has several rooms and courtyards on top. The Huaca del Sol is probably the largest adobe building in the Americas. In its present form it is 130 feet (40 m) high and about 1,150 feet (350) long. Originally it was much larger, but the sides have been damaged both by weather and by treasure hunters. It seems to have been built in a number of stages over several centuries. Its last building stage contained the grave of two people, but it may not have been built as a burial mound originally.

Both temples were probably used for religious ceremonies. Clues to this can be seen on Moche pots. Some show prisoners being sacrificed to fanged beings seated on top of pyramids.

▲ A gilded copper mask with shell-inlay eyes, found in a Moche burial. The ear lobes are stretched to take the large, decorative ear plugs worn by men of high rank.

▶ "Stirrup-spout" bottle showing the head of a Moche god. The fangs and curling snakes are reminders of the Chavín fanged god.

▼ Cerro Blanco towers over the Huaca de la Luna at Moche. The platform of adobe bricks rises about 70 ft (21 m). The rooms on top originally had painted wall designs.

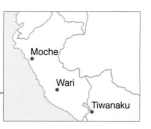

Tiwanaku and Wari

AROUND 650–1000 C.E. THESE TWO EMPIRES came to dominate much of the central and southern Andes and parts of the coast. The first is named after the ruins of Tiwanaku (Tiahuanaco) that lie in modern Bolivia, about 13 miles (20 km) east of Lake Titicaca.

The surrounding area, known as the *altiplano*, is a bleak treeless plateau. It is, however, the largest area of flat farming land in the Andes, and people have lived here for thousands of years.

Food plants such as potatoes and quinoa (a hardy grain) were probably first grown here. The land provides good grazing for llama and alpaca herds. In addition, the surrounding mountains are rich in gold, silver, copper, and tin.

Tiwanaku—a ceremonial center

Many of the great stone buildings at Tiwanaku seem to have been for ceremonial use. The most impressive are the Akapana, a large terraced pyramid, and the great temple enclosure known as the Kalasasaya.

At the northwest corner of the Kalasasaya is perhaps the best known of the monumental sculptures at Tiwanaku, the so-called Gateway of the Sun. The gateway, about 10 feet (3m) high, is cut from a single block of stone. At the top is a carved

▶ This sculptured figure stands just inside the Kalasasaya at Tiwanaku. It is carved from a single block of sandstone, 12 ft (4 m) high. The masklike face with its staring eyes is typical of the Tiwanaku art style.

▼ Lake Titicaca on the border of Bolivia and Peru. Situated at nearly 13,200 ft (4,000 m) above sea level, it is the highest navigable lake in the world. Here local fishermen use a type of ancient boat called a balsa. These boats are made of bundles of reeds bound together. Sails are made of cotton or of woven reed mats. The people of Tiwanaku used similar boats before the Spanish Conquest.

▼ Part of a wall of the huge sunken courtyard of the Kalasasaya, the largest and most important temple at Tiwanaku. One of the great gateways of Tiwanaku stands behind.

figure wearing a radiating headdress of puma heads. Condor and puma heads are carved on his body, and from his belt hangs a row of human faces, perhaps trophy heads from sacrificial victims.

Models for the Inca

The second civilization, Wari (Huari), was near the modern city of Ayacucho in the southern highlands of Peru. Stone carvings and pottery similar to those at Tiwanaku are found here, although they tend to be less elaborate.

The two civilizations, although about 400 miles (600 km) apart, were certainly in contact. They shared an art style and perhaps their religion, too. Both expanded their empires around the same time, becoming more powerful and conquering other territories. In their administrations, military organization, and communications, Tiwanaku and Wari were models for the later Inca state.

The Inca

UNTIL ABOUT 1440 THE INCA WERE ONLY one of several groups of people who were living in the southern Andes. By defeating their neighbors, they became the most powerful group. Under their great ruler, Pachacuti, the Inca began a campaign of conquest and rapidly expanded their territory, spreading north, south, and west. By the eve of the Spanish invasion in 1532 the Inca empire stretched nearly 2,500 miles (4,000 km) along the western coast of South America from northern Ecuador to central Chile.

Conquered territories

When a new region was conquered, an Inca noble of high rank was chosen to govern it. Local leaders were allowed to keep their posts as long as they remained loyal to the Inca emperor. Their children were taken as hostages to Cuzco, the Inca capital, where they were educated in Inca ways before returning home. Possible troublemakers were moved to other parts of the empire. Loyal colonists were brought in to replace them.

This policy of moving people about also meant that new ideas and ways of life were taken to other areas. Farming and irrigation methods, for example, were introduced by the Inca conquerors into regions where they had not existed before.

Governing the empire

Government of the Inca empire was organized like a pyramid, with the emperor, called Sapa Inca, at the top of the chain of command. The emperor was believed to be descended from the sun and was treated as a god. He had absolute power over his subjects. When he died his body was preserved in his

Growth of the Inca empire 1200–1532

1200 According to legend, the first Inca ruler, Manco Capac, comes to power and founds the city of Cuzco.

1438–63 Emperor Pachacuti extends the empire over highlands from Lake Titicaca in the southeast to Lake Junín in the northwest.

1463–71 Pachacuti's son, Topa Inca, conquers the lands along the north coast of Peru.

1471–93 Emperor Topa Inca extends the empire south to central Chile.

1493–1525 Emperor Huayna Capac extends the empire as far as Colombia.

1525 Incas first hear of white men in Panama.

1532 Spanish conquest of the Inca empire. Emperor Atahualpa killed.

▶ The Inca called their empire Tahuantinsuyu, meaning "Land of the Four Quarters." The quarters were: Chinchasuyu in the north, Cuntisuyu in the west, Antisuyu in the east, and Collasuyu in the south. At the center lay Cuzco, the Inca capital. To control their vast empire, the Inca built a great network of roads, often over difficult mountain terrain.

Extent of territory under Inca rulers
- Manco Capac c.1230
- Yahuar Huacac to c.1400
- Pachacuti 1438–63
- Pachacuti and Topa Inca 1463–71
- Topa Inca 1471–93
- Huayna Capac 1493–1525
- Inca empire 1525
- Boundary of empire quarter
- Inca road
- Inca town or city
- Important pre-Inca site
- Modern boundary

Scale 1 : 10 000 000
0   400 km
0   300 miles

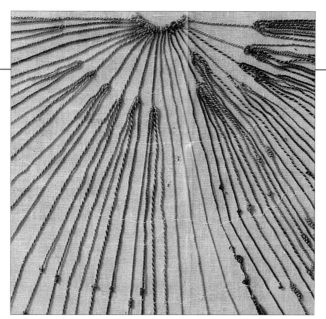

palace where servants continued to wait on him. At great festivals the mummies of long-dead Sapa Incas were carried in ceremonial procession through the streets of Cuzco.

Below the Sapa Inca were the governors of the four quarters of the empire and below them the governors of the provinces into which each quarter was divided. Underneath the provincial governors were local rulers and leaders. At the bottom were the ordinary people or commoners. Their lives were strictly controlled. They were not allowed to travel without official permission. Luxury goods, such as silver or gold objects, were reserved for the nobility.

Farming and work service

Most commoners were farmers. Each family in a community was given land according to its needs. Remaining fields were divided between the gods and the emperor. Farmers had to work these fields as well as their own.

The harvests from the religious and imperial fields were gathered into separate storehouses. Food from the religious storehouse fed the priests and provided offerings to the gods. Produce from the emperor's storehouse supported the nobles, the army, state officials, and craftsmen, as well as those who were too old or too sick to provide for themselves.

Each commoner had to do some work service for the government every year. Known as the *mit'a*, it could involve serving in the army, laboring in mines and quarries, or building and maintaining roads and bridges. Commoners belonged to kinship and land-sharing groups, in which each man's social status was fixed for life, unless he was rewarded by the emperor for some meritorious deed.

◀ These colored and knotted strings form a *quipu*, a system used by the Inca to keep records. Knots of different sizes represent different numbers. People called Quipucamayocs were specially trained to "read" the numbers. Andean herdsmen still use the *quipu* system to keep a record of their flocks.

▼ Inca cities had very efficient drainage and water-supply systems. A series of finely carved stone channels and basins carried water down through the mountain city of Machu Picchu. Shown here is one such channel.

◀ Remains of stonebuilt shrines at Tambomachay, east of Cuzco, show the skill of Inca stonemasons. The walls and terraces contain and channel a sacred spring (religious sites were built around springs from earliest times). The four niches at the top may represent caves from which, according to myth, the original Inca people emerged.

Cuzco—the great Inca capital

CUZCO WAS FOUNDED ABOUT 1200. In the 15th century the emperor Pachacuti changed it from a town of wood and thatch to a great stone city that enormously impressed the Spanish invaders. Present-day Cuzco is built on Inca remains. It is probably the oldest continuously occupied city in South America.

Cuzco was the hub of the Inca empire. A road system linked it to other Inca cities, villages, and relay stations. The "four quarters" into which the empire was divided radiated from Cuzco's central plaza, the Huacacapata.

The emperor's palace was the seat of government from which the empire was ruled. The Temple of the Sun was the Inca's most sacred shrine. Statues of the gods and other sacred objects were stored there. The walls were hung with elaborate tapestries and plated with gold and silver. Only priests and very important officials entered the temple. Most ceremonies were performed out of doors in the Huacacapata.

▲ Part of the Temple of the Sun can be seen beneath the church of Santo Domingo in Cuzco.

▼ Walls of Sacsahuaman, a fortress built above Cuzco. Fierce battles were fought here in the 1530s during the Spanish Conquest.

Machu Picchu
Cuzco

Machu Picchu

THE RUINS OF THE INCA CITY OF MACHU Picchu occupy one of the world's most spectacular ancient sites.

The city, about 43 miles (70 km) northwest of Cuzco, is built on a rocky ridge that is surrounded by high mountains. On either side the land slopes away in human-made terraces before dropping 2,000 feet (600 m) to the valley of the Urubamba River below. The city is visible on one side only—from a mountain road on the south. From the river valley it is completely invisible.

Mountain farmers

The ruins consist of nearly 300 buildings of stone arranged along the sides of an oblong plaza. Farming families lived in one-roomed houses grouped around a central courtyard. Inside, the houses would have been dark and smoky, but people would mostly have been outside in the courtyard or in the fields.

A stone aqueduct brought a supply of fresh water from the mountain streams. A system of channels and basins carried the water through the city and down to the farming terraces on the lower slopes.

Excellent builders in stone

The Inca were highly skilled architects, engineers, and stonemasons. Machu Picchu is the greatest example of their achievement in building in extremely difficult mountainous areas.

Stonemasons' tools consisted of stone and bronze chisels, hammers, and crowbars. Blocks of stone were worked into shape with hammers. The blocks were often rounded at the edges or polished so that they caught the light and made patterns.

The masons cut the blocks to fit so exactly that no mortar was needed to fasten them. The joints between the blocks are usually so tight that it is impossible to slip even a knife blade between them. Many Inca walls stand today, in spite of the earthquakes that shake the Andes.

◀ This view of Machu Picchu shows its dramatic mountain setting and the skillful way in which the builders used the natural contours of the site. Just visible are characteristic Inca doorways and niches. They are not perfectly rectangular in shape—they are narrower at the top than at the bottom.

Inca Travel

THE INCA NEEDED ROADS SO THEY COULD transport goods, move troops, and send messages. Without good roads it would have been almost impossible for them to govern their far-flung empire.

There were no wheeled vehicles in Peru (or anywhere else in pre-Conquest America). Goods had to be carried on people's backs or on llamas. Although roads were built in a straight line wherever possible, they could zigzag up steep slopes or they could be replaced by steps.

Travelers on the road

Government permission was needed by those who wished to use roads. Most people walked, but those of high rank were carried in litters. A 16th-century Spanish chronicler, Cieza de Leon, noted the splendor of emperors' travel:

> *"When the Incas visited the provinces of their empire in time of peace, they traveled in great majesty, seated in rich litters fitted with loose poles of excellent wood . . . enriched with gold and silver work . . . there were two high arches set with precious stones, and long mantles fell round all sides of the litter so as to cover it . . ."*

As well as officials, armies, and llama pack-trains on the roads, there were government messengers who provided a 24-hour service. Relay stations about 1 mile (1.6 km) apart housed a pair of runners. They received messages brought by runners from the previous station and carried them to the next. In this way, messages could be carried across the empire at a rate of about 150 miles (240 km) per day.

▶ Inca roads were often triumphs of engineering, especially in mountain areas. Sometimes their surface was paved. They were carried over rivers on bridges, over marshland on causeways, and occasionally through hills in tunnels. Here an important person is carried in a litter on the shoulders of four bearers.

Deep ravines were crossed by suspension bridges made of cables of twisted plant fibers. These bridges could be anything up to 200 ft (60 m) long. Although they swayed alarmingly in the wind, they seem to have been safe for foot travelers and pack animals. Some were in use until the 19th century.

▼ Tambo Colorado on the south coast of Peru. *Tambos*, or rest houses, were built along the roads for the use of official travelers. They were about a day's journey apart and they contained supplies of equipment, clothing, and food. Local communities were responsible for the upkeep of the *tambos* in their areas.

Andean Mummies and Textiles

NEW DISCOVERIES ABOUT THE INCA ARE still being made. In 2002 archaeologists found the ruins of a long-lost Inca stronghold at Cota Coca in the Vilcabamba region of Peru. The site contains about 40 stone buildings. It was probably a retreat for a "court in exile" following the Spanish Conquest and used until the fall of the last Inca emperor in 1572.

The Cotton King

Equally dramatic are finds of mummified human corpses. In a burial site at Puruchuco-Huaquerones near Lima, Peru, the mummified remains of thousands of people have been uncovered. One of the most impressive was the so-called Cotton King, a healthy male in his late 30s who had been laid to rest between 1480 and 1535.

The mummies reveal a cross section of Inca society, from very young to old. The burial site lies beneath a shantytown that has grown rapidly since the early 1990s. Waste water from the slums had begun to damage mummies, which for 500 years had lain undisturbed, preserved by bone-dry soil.

Clothed for the afterlife

Beautiful textiles and clothing were used by the ancient Peruvians as religious offerings and as gifts on special occasions, such as a baby's naming ceremony. When people died, quantities of textiles were buried with them.

Mummy bundles were first unearthed at the Lima site in 1956. However, no serious excavation was carried out until 1999. The Cotton King mummy—probably that of a noble—was wrapped in 300 pounds (136 kg) of raw cotton, along with the mummy of a baby. His grave goods for the afterlife included food (corn, sweet potatoes, and beans), together with pottery, a war club, a feathered headdress, and animal skins.

Mummies were given dummy heads of cloth stuffed with cotton. Faces were left blank, although some heads wore masks or wigs.

Sacrificial victims

Andean Americans made sacrifices of human victims on sacred mountain peaks. Three well-preserved bodies discovered on Mount Llullaillaco in Argentina may be those of children of subject rulers, sacrificed by the Incas on the mountaintop, where the extreme cold and thin air have preserved the corpses well enough for DNA samples to be taken.

▼ A piece of mummy cloth from a Paracas mummy bundle. The design is a symbolic decoration intended to protect the wearer in the afterlife.

▶ A man's cap of woven wool shaped with a point at each corner. Such caps are typical of Wari–Tiwanaku ceremonial costume. They are shown in pottery and carving.

▶ (Far right) Feathers were attached to a backing of woven cotton to make ceremonial garments such as this neckpiece (from Peru, c.1200–1470 C.E.).

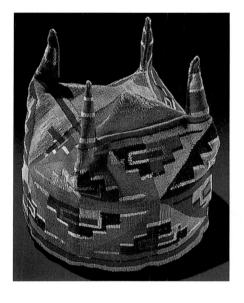

Textiles in Andean history

People have made cloth in Peru for at least 6,000 years. The earliest textiles were made from wild cotton, and people began planting this crop around 3500 B.C.E.

Later, the glossy wool of the domesticated llama and alpaca were used, as well as the finer, silkier fleece of the wild vicuña that lives on the Andean plateau. Most dyes came from plants, and as many as 200 colors are used in designs in the Paracas embroideries (see pages 76–77).

Most people wore a loose sleeveless tunic. Inca tunics were sometimes made from one piece of cloth with a slit in the center for the wearer's head. Both men and women wore cloaks, fastened with a large pin. Feather decoration and headbands denoted high rank. The emperor wore a special headband hung with red tassels.

Women did most of the weaving, and often had their spinning and weaving tools buried with them. Under Inca law, the wife of a commoner had to provide one woven garment a year as part of her family's tax payment to the emperor. Noblewomen, even the wife or daughter of the emperor, were taught to weave and spin as part of their education for the priesthood or marriage.

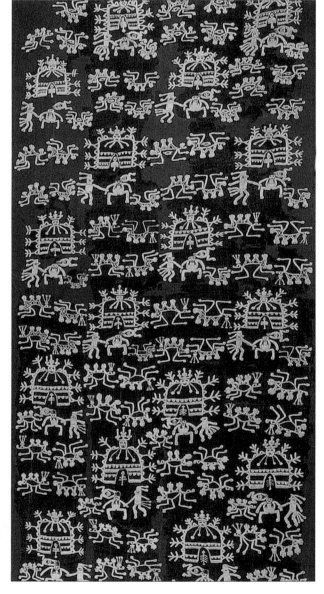

◀ This cotton mantle with wool embroidery showing supernatural beings probably wrapped a body for burial.

▼ A mummy wrapped in embroidered cloth from Paracas. The desert conditions preserved it for 2,000 years.

Latin America Today

IN LATIN AMERICA MANY ASPECTS OF THE ancient way of life continue to survive. For example, buildings are still constructed using traditional materials such as stone, cane, and adobe. In the highlands of Peru houses are still thatched with the same grass as they were in Inca times.

Many of the foodstuffs that people in Latin America eat today are direct descendants of those grown thousands of years ago. Although wheat and barley are grown nowadays, corn remains the most important crop and of course has spread to other parts of the world. There are a number of Native American foods that have been brought to Europe over the centuries and have become familiar items in our own diet. As well as corn, these foods include potatoes, tomatoes, pineapples, avocados, several kinds of beans and peppers, peanuts, and chocolate.

The Spanish introduced several new domestic animals into the Americas. In the Andes, for

▶ Inca farmers harvested potatoes and made holes for planting seed using a foot plow. This was like a curved digging stick with a foot rest near the pointed end. Here, present-day farmers are seen using foot plows to break up the ground on a farming terrace in Peru. These tools have been shown to suit shallow soil better than modern mechanical plows.

◀ During the Incas' rule of their empire, markets were held in each district where local people could exchange their surplus produce and goods such as fruit, vegetables, or pottery. Peruvian villagers today still hold markets on ancient Inca sites. The one shown here takes place once a week at Chinchero, a town near Cuzco. The goods on display are much the same as those bartered in Inca times. Women still carry their produce or purchases in large cloths on their backs, just as their ancestors did.

▶ The first Native Americans seen by Columbus were "all naked and painted white, red, black." Amazon Indians still paint their bodies on special occasions. Here two Yanomamo women decorate each other for a feast using paint made from plants.

▼ The Tarahumara Indians of northern Mexico perform the Dance of the Pharisees during Holy Week (the week before Easter). They paint their bodies and wear chicken or turkey feather crowns. They dance with a straw effigy of Judas, who betrayed Jesus.

example, llamas have been largely replaced by sheep for meat and wool, and by donkeys as pack animals. Alpacas are still kept for their wool, since weaving continues both for the Native Americans' own use and for the tourist trade. Many weavers, however, find it easier to buy ready-spun yarn or to use chemical dyes that produce brighter colors than plant dyes.

Rituals and sacred places

Traditional religion became interwoven with Christianity, giving a distinctive texture to Roman Catholic observances. Jesus Christ is often identified with the old sun god and the Virgin Mary with the moon goddess (by the Maya) or with the earth goddess (in the Andes). On feast days people carry statues of the Christian saints through the streets just as they carried statues of the gods in pre-Conquest times.

▲ Modern Native American clothing is sometimes a mixture of Native American and Spanish colonial styles. These town officers in the Mexican state of Chiapas wear Native American ponchos over European-style shirts and trousers.

Like their ancestors, some present-day Native Americans also believe in the supernatural power of certain places or objects. Caves, rocks, trees, and streams are often seen as holy places, and offerings are made to the gods who inhabit them.

In some regions of the Andes, sacred cloth bundles are still displayed at annual ceremonies to bless crops and livestock. They are then rewrapped and hidden until the following year.

Survival of ancient customs is precarious, however, where sites and communities are threatened by environmental change and the incursion of the modern world.

Glossary

adobe Sun-dried mud-bricks, used for building houses.

agave A type of cactus. It was used as a food and to make an alcoholic drink.

cactus A prickly desert plant, characterized by large, tough stems, brightly colored flowers, and leaves reduced to spines or scales.

chinampa A small plot of land reclaimed from the mud of lakes in Central Mexico. The plots were used for growing crops.

conquistadores A Spanish word for "conquerors." It is usually applied to the Spanish conquerors of Mexico and Peru in the 16th century.

copal A hard aromatic yellow, orange, or red resin from various tropical trees. It was used in varnishes as well as for incense.

gorget A breast ornament of stone, shell, or metal with holes for wearing on a cord around the neck.

hunters and gatherers People who live by hunting animals and gathering wild plants for food.

Ice Age A period of cold climate when much of Earth's surface was covered with ice. There were, in fact, several Ice Ages. The last one began about 70,000 years ago and ended only about 10,000 years ago.

Inuit (Eskimo) The inhabitants of the Arctic coasts and islands. There are two main groups: the Yupik who inhabit eastern Siberia and southern and central Alaska, and the Inuit who stretch from northern Alaska to Greenland. In Canada Inuit (meaning "people") has come to replace "Eskimo," the name given by neighboring Native Americans and later adopted by Europeans.

Iroquois A term usually restricted to the Native American groups who allied to form the League of the Iroquois in the 16th century: the Seneca, Cayuga, Onondaga, Oneida, Mohawk, and Tuscarora.

Iroquoian A term referring to all Native American groups speaking Iroquoian languages.

litter A vehicle in the form of a chair or couch carried on poles on people's shoulders.

mesquite A thorny shrub bearing edible beanlike pods. It grows in Mexico and the southwestern United States.

mestizo The name given in Latin America to a person of mixed Native American and European descent.

mica A mineral-bearing rock that can be split into thin transparent sheets.

mummy The remains of a dead person preserved in accordance with traditional religious belief.

native A local inhabitant of a country. In America the term refers to the American Indians. Today many American Indians prefer to be called Native Americans.

nomadic The term used to describe those who wander from place to place, usually in search of food.

Norse The people of ancient Scandinavia, especially Norway.

prehistoric The term used to describe the period in history before the appearance of written records.

In American Indian history this is usually taken to mean before 1492 (the year Columbus arrived).

quetzal bird A Central American bird of the pheasant family, prized for its brightly colored feathers.

sarcophagus A stone coffin, often decorated with sculpture or carving.

semidesert Land that is very dry but where it is still possible for some plants to grow for part of the year at least.

stirrup-spout A hollow handle and spout in the shape of a stirrup (a horserider's footrest). A typical feature of Moche pottery.

supernatural Beyond the ordinary forces of nature, to do with gods and other mysterious beings.

travois A wheelless vehicle used by the Plains Indians of North America to carry their belongings, consisting of a V-shaped framework of poles fastened to an animal's back and dragged along the ground behind it. It was pulled by dogs and (after about 1700) by horses.

FURTHER READING

Books for young people
Coe, M. *The Maya* (Thames & Hudson, 2005).
Fagan, B. *Ancient North America* (Thames & Hudson, 2004).
Isaacs, S. S. *America in the Time of Columbus* (Heinemann Library Chicago, 1998).
Isaacs, S. S. *Picture the Past: Life in a Hopi Village* (Heinemann Library Chicago, 2001).
McEwan, C., Barretto, C., and E. G. Neves (eds.). *The Unknown Amazon* (British Museum Press, 2001.)
Machado, A. M. *Exploration Into Latin America* (Belitha, 1996).
Williams, B. (ed.). *The Atlas of Human History: Civilizations of the Americas* (Cherrytree Books, 1996).
Younkin, P. *Indians of the Arctic and Subarctic* (Facts On File, 1992).

Reference books for adults
Katz, F. *The Ancient American Civilizations* (Phoenix Giant, 1997).
Moseley, M. E. *The Incas and Their Ancestors* (Thames & Hudson, 2001).

Myths and legends
Clark, E. E. *Indian Legends of the Pacific Northwest* (University of California, 1958).
Gifford, D. *Warriors, Gods and Spirits from Central and South American Mythology* (Schocken Books, 1983).

Nungak, Z., and E. Arima. *Eskimo Stories/Unikkaatuat* (Ottawa, 1969).
Wood, M. *Spirits, Heroes, and Hunters from North American Indian Mythology* (Schocken Books, 1982).

Useful Web sites
http://www.cahokiamounds.com/cahokia.html
Resources on Cahokia.

http://www.cr.nps.gov
National Parks Service "links to the past."

http://www.famsi.org
Resources on Mesoamerican civilizations.

http://www.head-smashed-in.com
Head-Smashed-In buffalo jump and rock art site, Alberta, Canada.

http://www.huacas.com/page170.htm
Resources on the Moche pyramids, and links.

http://www.nmai.si.edu
National Museum of the American Indian, Washington, DC.

http://www.socioambiental.org/pib/indexenglish.htm
Resources and information on indigenous peoples in Brazil.

Gazetteer

The gazetteer lists places and features, such as islands or mountains, found on the maps. Each has a separate entry including a page and grid reference number. For example:
Adena 25 D3

All features are shown in *italic* type. For example: *Aconcagua, mt.* 9 D2

A letter after the feature describes the kind of feature:
d. district; *i.* island; *isls.* islands; *mt.* mountain; *mts.* mountains; *r.* river

Abaj Takalik 54 C1, 57 E5, 63 B2
Abitibi Narrows 18 F3
Acolhuacan, d. 70 B3
Aconcagua, mt. 9 D2
Adena 25 D3
Adena Park 25 D3
Agua Dulce 75 B2
Alabama, r. 25 C2, 27 C2
Alaska Range, mts. 9 A7
Aleutian Islands 20 A2
Alibates 18 C2
Altar de Sacrificios 54 C2
Amazon, r. 9 E3, 13 E3
Amazonia, d. 13 D3
Ambato 82 B8
Ameca 67 A3
Ammassalik 21 H3
Anaktuvuk Pass 20 B3
Ancohuma, mt. 9 D3
Andes, mts. 9 D3, 82 B7
Andrews 18 E3
Angel 27 C3
Antilles, d. 13 D4
Antilles, Greater, isls. 75 B3
Antilles, Lesser, isls. 9 E4, 75 D3
Antisuyu, d. 82 D6
Antonio Plaza 57 C2
Apatzingan 67 A2
Appalachian Mountains 9 D5, 25 D3, 27 D3
Araguaia, r. 9 E3
Arctic, d. 13 C7
Arkansas, r. 25 B3, 27 B3
Armadillo 54 B3
Armstrong 18 D3
Arroyo Sonso 57 C2
Arzberger 32 D2
Asunción 9 E2
Asunción Mita 63 C2
Atazta 67 C2
Atico 82 C5
Atlan, d. 70 C4
Atotonilco, d. 70 B4
Atotonilco, d. 70 B3
Axocopan, d. 70 B4
Aztalan 27 C4

Baffin Island 9 D7, 13 D7, 21 G3
Bahamas, isls. 13 D5
Balancán 57 E6
Balsas, r. 54 A2, 67 B2, 70 A3
Barriles 75 B2
Bat Cave 18 C2
Baum 27 D3
Bedford 25 B3
Bell 21 E3
Belmopan 9 D4
Beluga Point 20 B3
Bent 18 F3
Betanci 75 B2

Big Hidatsa 32 C3
Bighorn Medicine Wheel 32 B2
Big Sycamore 36 B1
Birch 18 E3
Birnirk 20 B4
Blackduck 27 B5
Bloody Falls 21 D3
Bogotá 9 D4
Bonampak 63 B3
Boone 25 B4
Borax Cave 18 A2
Boucher 25 F4
Bowmans Brook 27 F4
Brand 18 D2
Brasilia 9 E3
Brazilian Highlands 9 E3
Brohm 18 E3
Brooks River 20 B2
Bryce Canyon 36 C2
Buchanan 21 E3
Buenos Aires 9 E2
Buritaca 75 C2
Bynum 25 C2

Cahokia 27 B3
Cajamarca 82 B7
Calakmul 63 C4
Calima, d. 75 B1
Calixtlahuaca 67 B2
Campbell Mound 25 D4
Canapote 75 B2
Capacha 54 A2
Caracas 9 D4
Cascade Range, mts. 9 B6, 36 A3
Catarpe 82 D4
Cato 25 C3
Cempoala 67 B2, 70 C3
Cerro de la Bomba 54 B2
Chalcatzinco 54 B2, 57 D6
Chalchihuites 67 A3
Chalchuapa 54 D1, 57 E5
Chalco, d. 70 B3
Chalk Hollow 18 C2
Chance 27 F4
Chan Chan 82 B7
Chapultepec 67 B2
Chavín de Huantar 82 B7
Chiapa de Corzo 54 C2
Chichén Itzá 63 C5, 67 D3
Chicnimeca Desert 67 A3
Chilecito 82 D3
Chinchasuyu, d. 82 B7
Chiquihuitillo 67 A3
Chiquitoy 82 B7
Chirikof Island 20 B2
Choris 20 B3
Chucalissa 27 C3
Chucuito 82 D5
Chugachik Island 20 B3
Chupicuaro 54 A3
Chuquiabo 82 D5
Ciénaga de Oro 75 B2
Cihuatlan, d. 70 A2
Circum Caribbean, d. 13 D4
Claiborne 18 E2
Clasons Point 27 F4
Clay Mound 27 D3
Clemsons Island 27 E4
Coast Mountains 9 B6, 48 C2
Coast Range, mts. 48 D1
Coatzacoalcos, r. 57 A1, 57 B2
Cobá 63 D5
Coixtlahuacan, d. 70 C2
Cojumatlan 67 A3
Collasuyu, d. 82 D4
Colorado, r. 36 C2
Columbia, r. 36 A4, 48 D1
Comalcalco 63 A4
Comitán 54 C2
Copán 54 D1, 63 C2

Copiapo 82 C3
Cow Point 18 G3
Coxcatlan Cave 54 B2
Coyolapan, d. 70 C2
Crab Orchard 25 C3
Craig Harbour 21 F4
Crespo 75 B2
Criel Mound 25 D3
Crow Creek 32 D2
Cruz del Milagro 57 A2
Crystall II 21 G3
Cuahuacan, d. 70 B3
Cuauhnahuac, d. 70 B3
Cuauhtitlan, d. 70 B3
Cuauhtochco, d. 70 C3
Cuba, i. 13 D5
Cuetlaxtlan, d. 70 C3
Cueva Humida 54 B3
Culhuacan 67 B2
Cuntisuyu, d. 82 C6
Cuzco 13 D3, 82 C6

Dalles, The 18 A3
Danger Cave 18 B3, 36 C3
Davis 27 B2
Death Valley 36 B2
de Blicquy 21 E4
Deer Canyons 36 B1
Deltatefrasserne 21 H5
Diablo 54 B3
Diana Bay 21 F3
Dickson 27 D4
Dirty Shame Rockshelter 36 B3
Dismal Lake 21 D3
Dodemansbugten 21 I4
Dodge Island 48 B2
Doerschuk 18 F2
Dorset, Cape 21 F3
Double Adobe 18 C2
Double Ditch 32 C3
Double House Village 36 B4
Dripping Springs 36 B1
Drunken Point 18 E3
Dundas Island 21 E4
Dust Devil 18 B2
Dyer 18 E3
Dzibilchaltún 54 D3, 63 C5

Eastern Highlands, d. 13 E3
Eastern Prairie 32 D3
Eastern Subarctic, d. 13 D6
Eastern Woodlands, d. 13 C6, 32 E3
Ecdzná 63 B4
El Baúl 63 B2
El Cafetal 75 B2
El Chayal 54 C1
El Indio 75 B2
Elk Island 18 D4
Ellis Landing 36 A2
El Mesón 56 A4
El Mirador 63 C3
El Opeño 54 A3
El Teul 67 A3
El Viejón 57 D6
Emerald Mound 27 B2
Emeryville Shellmound 36 A2
Engigstciak 20 C3
Esilao 48 D1
Estero Rabón 57 B2
Etowah 27 D2
Eva 18 E2

Fanning 32 D1
Fisher 27 D4
Five Mile Rapids 36 A4, 48 D1
Florence 27 C2
Fort Ancient 25 D3
Fort Walton 27 C2
Fraser, r. 48 D2

Galápagos Islands 9 C3
Gargamelle Cove 21 G2
Garoga 27 F4
Gatecliff Shelter 36 B2
Georgetown 9 E4
Glacier Bay 48 A3
Gods Lake 18 D4
Goodall 25 C4
Graham Cave 18 D2
Gran Chaco, d. 13 D2
Grand Rapids 18 D4
Grand Village 27 B2
Grave Creek Mound 25 D3
Great Basin 9 C6, 13 C6, 36 B3
Great Plains 9 C6
Greenland, i. 13 E7, 21 H4
Grijalva, r. 63 A3, 70 E2
Guatavita 75 C1
Guatemala City 9 C4
Guayabo de Turrialba 75 B2
Guiana Highlands 9 D4
Guida Farm 27 F4
Gulf Hazard 21 F2

Hardaway 18 E2
Hathaway 18 G3
Hatuncolla 82 D5
Havana 9 D5
Havana 25 C4
Hickson Petroglyph 36 B2
High Plains 32 C2
Hispaniola, i. 13 D4, 75 C3
Hiwassee Island 27 D3
Hogup Cave 18 B3, 36 C3
Hoko River 48 D1
Hooper Bay 20 B3
Hopewell 25 D3
Horn, Cape 9 D1
Howard Lake 25 B4
Huahuco 82 B7
Huancabamba 82 B7
Huaxtepec, d. 70 B3
Huaylas 82 B7
Huber 27 D4
Huehuetenango 54 C2
Hueipochtlan, d. 70 B4
Huff 32 C3
Hungary Hall 18 D3

Iceland, i. 13 F7, 21 I3
Igloolik 21 F3
Illinois, r. 27 C4
Illummersuit 21 G4
Illutalik 21 H3
Imaha 21 F3
Incawasi 82 B6
Indian Knoll 18 E2
Ingapirca 82 B8
Inglefield Land 21 G4
Inussuk 21 G4
Inverhuron 18 E3
Ipiutak 20 B3
Islona de Chantuto 54 C2
Itinnera 21 G3
Itztepetl 67 A3
Ixtlan 67 A3
Iyatayet 20 B3
Izamal 63 C5, 67 D3
Izapa 54 C1, 57 E5, 63 A2

Jackson 21 D4
Jaina 63 B5
Jaketown 18 D2, 25 B2
Japurá, r. 9 D3
Jauja 82 B6
Joss 21 D4
Juxtlahuaca 54 B2, 57 D6

Kabah 63 C5
Kaminaljuyu 63 B2

Kangeq 21 G3
Kap Holbaek 21 I5
Karlo Site 36 A3
Kathio 27 B5
Kelso 27 E4
Kemp 27 D3
Key Marco 27 D1
Kings Beach 36 A2
Kings Mounds 27 C3
Knapp Mounds 27 B3
Knight 25 B3
Kolnaes Umiak 21 I5
Kolomoki 27 D2
Koster 18 D2
Kukak 20 B2
Kurigitavik 20 B3
Kuujjua River 21 D4

Labná 63 C5
Labrador 9 D6, 13 D6
Lady Franklin Point 21 D3
Laguna de los Cerros 54 B2, 57 A3
La Honradez 63 C3
La India 75 B2
La Jolla 18 B2
Lake Jackson 27 D2
Lake Mohave 18 B2
Lamar 27 D2
Lamoka Lake 18 F3
L'Anse aux Meadows 13 E6
La Paya 82 D3
La Paz 9 D3
La Perra 54 B3
La Quemada 67 A3
Las Bocas 57 D6
Las Flores 67 B3
Las Limas 57 A1
Las Victorias 54 D1
Latacunga 82 B8
La Venta 57 C3
Leary 32 D2
Leeward Islands 75 D3
Le Montaña 75 B2
Leó 67 A3
Lima 9 D3, 13 D3
Little Harbor Site 18 B2
Little Sycamore 36 B1
Logan Creek 18 D3
Lonesome Creek 21 G5
Los Idolos 57 B2
Los Mangos 57 A3
Los Remedios 67 B2
Los Soldados 57 C3
Los Tapiales 54 C2
Lovelock Cave 36 B3
Lower Hidatsa 32 C3
Lubaantun 63 C3

McConnell 18 E3
Machaquilá 63 C3
Machu Picchu 82 C6
McKean 18 C3
Mackenzie, r. 9 B7, 21 D3
Mackenzie Mountains 9 B7
McKinley, Mount 9 A7
Madeira, r. 9 D3
Madira Bickel Mound 27 D1
Magdalena, r. 75 C2
Maimisburg 25 D3
Malaga Cove 36 B1
Malambo 75 C2
Malerualik 21 E3
Malinalco, d. 70 B3
Mammoth Creek 36 B2
Managua 9 D4
Mani 54 D3
Mann 25 C3
Marañón, r. 82 E8
Marcey Creek 18 F2

93

Index